ISBN-13: 979-8-9996477-0-2

I0143381

Praise For Putting A Smile On The Face Of God

In a culture of hustle, noise, constant striving, and superficial spirituality, Rich Rollins offers a better way: a quiet, faithful walk with God marked by trust, obedience, and joy. *Putting a Smile on the Face of God* brings clarity to the confusion many who follow Jesus feel about God's will, spiritual growth, and what it really means to live a life that honors God. Every chapter is grounded in scripture, practical wisdom and lived experience. Reading this book felt like having coffee with a spiritual mentor —someone who's walked the road ahead, who remembers the questions we wrestle with and who lovingly points you towards the everyday habits that reflect God's heart and produce a life that pleases God.

Jack Anthony Sheets, Pastor, Cityline Church

There is so much gold in this book! For instance, the insight into the different types of God's will is life-changing in how you'll process decisions and change. There is so much grace and practical encouragement throughout, all rooted in profound biblical insights. This is a great book!

Alex Absalom, Dandelion Resourcing)

DEDICATION

*To my grandchildren, Lily, David, and
Charlie Dickson. May they discover the life
of their dreams in pleasing the Lord.*

Putting A Smile

On The

Face Of God

*Simple Habits for a Life
that Pleases Jesus*

Dr. Rich Rollins

ProBiblica Publishers

CONTENTS

INTRODUCTION

May the words of my mouth and the meditation of my heart
be pleasing in your sight, O Lord, my Rock and my Redeemer.
(Psalm 19:14)

Over the past few decades, I have been blessed to serve thousands of individuals seeking a better life. As a pastor, people turn to me for spiritual guidance, seeking God's will in their relationships, careers, finances, health, and daily routines. Most are pursuing the life they have always dreamed of.

I've always been amazed at how surprised many people are when they realize that salvation doesn't automatically bring happiness. Being rescued from darkness and brought into the Kingdom of Light creates new tensions between the old worldview and God's Spirit-led perspective. Soon after salvation, new battles begin. Suffering doesn't stop. Jake's (not his real name) story illustrates these tensions. He was a biker living a life full of crime, drugs, and rebellion. A friend who once shared his lifestyle introduced him to the gospel. His life and outlook changed when he accepted Jesus as his personal Savior. He no longer wanted to "hang out with the gang." During the first months of his new life, he experienced a mix of inner peace and chaos on every level. A fresh sense of peace and contentment entered his life, even as his friends criticized him for abandoning their friendship. The woman he had lived with for over ten years, with whom he had two children, rejected his new way of life and wanted to keep partying with other bikers. After several months of daily conflict, she asked Jake to move out. When he resisted, she obtained a restraining order preventing him from seeing her or the "kids." Since they never married, the law gave her full rights to the children. He lost his relationship with his partner and kids; no one wanted anything to do with him, leaving him feeling miserable and alone. Sitting in my office, Jake began listing all his problems, blaming his conversion to Christianity for them. He believed accepting Jesus as his Savior would bring him peace and happiness. He did feel peace and joy, but soon realized his decision had brought new, unexpected conflicts. He wondered where the abundant life Jesus promised was. The enemy was tempting him to believe he had traded one life of misery for another.

The enemy tries to deceive us into thinking that Christianity is just another bait-and-switch tactic. He claims that God's offer promises happiness, only for us to find that our choices have brought us misery. He argues that if God truly loved us, we would be more satisfied. Satan is a liar. The promises of Christianity in the Bible are honest and genuine. Being rescued from darkness brings eternal rewards and present joy. Our rescue also begins a lifelong journey of walking in the Spirit as we develop habits that bring us closer to God and His plan for our lives. Only by beginning this journey will we start to experience complete joy, peace, and wonder in the Christian life. We will then come to understand God's unconditional love. It took Jake several years of spiritual growth before he started to feel the peace and joy that come from knowing God. Those years were spent honoring God by building new habits.

Many people confuse God's love with His approval of us. God's love for us is unconditional, limitless, and steady. It stays the same no matter what we do or what happens around us. The true sign of His love isn't seen in our present condition but in the historical fact that He sent His Son for our salvation. Just because He loves us doesn't mean God approves of everything we do. People feel happy with us when we meet their expectations, but we can be loved by others even if they are not pleased with us. This also shows how God relates to us. It's a mistake to think that God's love is the same as His approval. The proof of God's love is shown in Jesus's sacrifice for us. God can love us without always taking pleasure in us. Therefore, the goal of the Christian life is to live in a way that pleases God.

Pleasing my dad meant being obedient and meeting his expectations. Although I rarely admitted it, most of his expectations were realistic and achievable. Making my dad happy was a top priority. What child doesn't want to please their parent? Just as pleasing our earthly fathers matters, pleasing God also involves meeting His expectations, which is even more critical. Throughout Scripture, we see God's guidance for His children about His expectations and the promise that pleasing Him leads to a better life. This is why Paul emphasizes the importance of pleasing the Lord.

So we make it our goal to please him, whether we are at home in the body or away from it. (2 Corinthians 5:9)

For you were once darkness, but now you are light in the Lord. Live as children of light (for the fruit of the light consists in all goodness, righteousness and truth) and find out what pleases the Lord. (Ephesians 5:8-11)

Finally, brothers, we instructed you how to live in order to please God, as in fact you are living. Now we ask you and urge you in the Lord Jesus to do this more and more. For you know what instructions we gave you by the authority of the Lord Jesus. (1 Thessalonians 4:1-2)

My friend Jake expected joy from finding Jesus, but he was quickly surprised by how rapidly his situation changed. Many believers who have been saved for years experience similar feelings as they long for the abundant life Jesus promises. Many of us struggle with feeling "OK" with God. When we stumble, the enemy whispers that because of our failure, God no longer loves us. Sometimes we hear, "Your behavior proves that you are not God's child." Like all half-truths, there is some truth to Satan's temptation. The truth is: God feels disappointed when we fail to please Him. He still loves us but grieves when we refuse to obey His word. He is hurt when our lives lack the spiritual habits that strengthen our relationship with Him. Those who please God with their lives demonstrate a Christian life built on following the right path and developing spiritual habits that nurture their relationship with their Creator. These believers experience the life they've always wanted—the life they hoped for when they first met Jesus. This book aims to guide you toward fulfillment and contentment in the Christian life. This path is found by aligning our walk with God's will and trusting Him. We will experience the life we've always desired when we follow this journey.

Considering this topic, we have organized our thoughts around Paul's prayer in Colossians 1:9-14.

> *For this reason, since the day we heard about you, we have not stopped praying for you and asking God to fill you with the knowledge of his will through all spiritual wisdom and understanding. And we pray this in order that you may live a life worthy of the Lord and may please him in every way...*

Paul openly emphasizes the importance of pleasing God. In his prayer, he outlines the path to pleasing Him and describes what a fulfilling life involves. This book centers on what it takes to please God and highlights the primary purpose of life: living in a way that honors and delights the Creator. In a world filled with distractions and conflicting messages about success, identity, and fulfillment, understanding what pleases God provides clarity, peace, and guidance. This book can help readers understand what God desires for their lives and how their daily choices reflect their love for Him. Knowing and following God's will strengthens our relationship, creates a meaningful life, and prepares believers to hear the ultimate praise: "Well done, good and faithful servant" (Matthew 25:21).

Reflect & Respond

As you finish this chapter, take a few quiet moments to reflect on what God might be speaking to your heart. These questions help you remember key truths, deepen your understanding, challenge your assumptions, and motivate you to action.

Whether you're working through them alone or with a group, invite the Holy Spirit to guide your thoughts, encourage honest conversations, and reveal the next step in your walk with Christ. Let this be not just a review but a response of faith, obedience, and transformation.

1. What misconceptions do people often hold about the Christian life after salvation, and how do these misunderstandings affect their spiritual growth?

2. What is the difference between being loved by God and living in a way that pleases Him? In what ways can these concepts be confused, and have you personally struggled with this tension?

3. How do spiritual habits shape our experience of the life that God intends for His children, and are you nurturing any of these habits in your own life?

4. How does the example of pleasing an earthly father help illustrate what it means to please God, and what insights does this analogy provide for your relationship with Him?

5. What does it mean to you to "live a life worthy of the Lord" (Colossians 1:10), and how might this understanding influence your daily decisions and your current walk with God?

CHAPTER ONE

WHY PLEASE GOD?

True faith rests in the will of God. Our greatest
pleasure should be to please Him.
A.W. Tozer

If you are pleased with me,
teach me your ways so I may know you
and continue to find favor with you.
(Ex 33:13)

Pleasing the Lord is vital for faith, righteous living, and finding the life we all desire. Moses recognized this when he pleaded with the Lord in Exodus 33. Sadly, many people expect to achieve their dreams without effort and obedience, neglecting to try to please the Lord. We often wrongly assume that God's approval is automatic because of His love for us. While He does love us, His pleasure comes from our obedience. Reaching the life we want depends on His love and our willingness to please Him. Many confuse the American Dream with the life God intends for us, which is very different from what He plans. Most of us pursue growth, progress, and happiness without making the necessary changes that lead to a better, God-ordained life. Obedience demands that we bend and submit to God's will, which can be tough. Often, we long for a life that differs greatly from what our Creator designed, especially among American believers.

The Christianization of the American Dream has hidden God's plan for us as His children, made in His image. We are deceived by a false message that promises a good job, financial freedom, a beautiful home, a healthy bank account, a secure retirement, and other parts of the American Dream that are meant to bring happiness. While achieving these goals might make us appear successful in America, they do not provide the deep contentment and purpose that God offers. Chasing the American Dream often leaves us feeling empty. The life we truly need and desire can only come from pleasing the Lord. When we dedicate ourselves to pleasing Him, He is pleased with us. Our sincerity is evident in eight key areas.

Obedience to God's Commandments: The Bible often links pleasing God with following His commandments. Jesus said, "If you love me, keep my commandments" (John 14:15). Obedience demonstrates our love and respect for God and is marked by sincerity, which makes us trustworthy to those around us.

We know that we have come to know him if we obey his commands. The man who says, "I know him," but does not do what he commands is a liar, and the truth is not in him. But if anyone obeys his word, God's love is truly made complete in him. This is how we know we are in him: Whoever claims to live in him must walk as Jesus did. (1 John 2:3-6)

Faith: Hebrews 11:6 states, "And without faith it is impossible to please God because anyone who comes to him must believe that he exists and that he rewards those who earnestly seek him." Faith in God and His promises is essential for pleasing Him. Peter reminds us that through faith we are shielded by God's power (1 Peter 1:5). Faithful people "win favor and a good name in the sight of God and man." (Proverbs 3:3). Those who please God show the habits that come with trusting Him in everything.

Righteous Living: Living a life of righteousness and holiness pleases the Lord. Romans 12:1-2 urges believers to present their bodies as a living sacrifice, holy and pleasing to God, and not to conform to the patterns of this world but to be transformed by the renewal of their minds. Those who live righteously are like trees planted by the river's edge, yielding fruit in season (Psalm 1). They thrive in all their endeavors.

Love and Compassion: The Bible emphasizes that love and compassion toward others are pleasing to God. Jesus taught that the greatest commandments are to love God and to love your neighbor (Matthew 22:37-40). John reminds believers that humanity can only see the unseen God by loving others. Through this, we reveal God.

> *No one has ever seen God; but if we love one another, God lives in us and his love is made complete in us. (1 John 4:12)*

Seeking God's Will: Pleasing God involves pursuing and obeying His will. Colossians 1:10 states, "So that you may live a life worthy of the Lord and please Him in every way: bearing fruit in every good work, growing in the knowledge of God." Christians are universally motivated to follow God's will. Those who please the Lord experience it in tangible ways, reflected in a fulfilling life.

Spiritual Sacrifices: Developing the habit of offering spiritual sacrifices, such as prayer, praise, and thanksgiving, pleases God. Hebrews 13:15-16 encourages believers to present a sacrifice of praise to God regularly and to do good while sharing with others. Those who please God see their world through His heart and eyes, as demonstrated throughout the Scriptures.

Moral Integrity: Living honestly and avoiding sin pleases the Lord. Proverbs 11:20 states, "The Lord detests those whose hearts are perverse, but he delights in those whose ways are blameless."

Trust and Dependence on God: Having faith in God's guidance and relying on His strength pleases Him. Proverbs 3:5-6 states, "Trust in the Lord with all your heart and lean not on your understanding; in all your ways submit to him, and he will make your paths straight." These traits are evident in everyone who seeks to please God. As children of God, they develop habits that bring them closer to the Lord who saved them. By living transformed lives, they reap the rewards of pleasing God. Scripture highlights many blessings and benefits that come from bringing joy to Him. Here are a few.

Favor and Blessings: Pleasing God results in receiving His favor and blessings. Proverbs 16:7 states, "When the Lord takes pleasure in anyone's way, he causes their enemies to make peace with them."

Answered Prayers: Those who seek to please God can expect their prayers to be heard and answered. 1 John 3:22 states, "And we will receive from him whatever we ask because we obey him and do the things that please him."

Peace and Joy: Living a life that pleases God brings inner peace and happiness. Psalm 37:4 encourages, "Take delight in the Lord, and he will give you the desires of your heart."

May the God of hope fill you with all joy and peace as you trust in him, so that you may overflow with hope by the power of the Holy Spirit. (Romans 15:13)

Spiritual Growth: Pleasing the Lord encourages spiritual development and maturity. Colossians 1:10 highlights this by stating, "So that you may live a life worthy of the Lord and please him in every way: bearing fruit in every good work, growing in the knowledge of God."

Divine Guidance: Those who please God can expect His guidance. Proverbs 3:5-6 assures us, "Trust in the Lord with all your heart and lean not on your own understanding; in all your ways submit to him, and he will make your paths straight." The decisions of the wise differ profoundly from those of the foolish or immature. The immature expend energy trying to determine right from wrong, while the mature wrestle with choosing between what is better and what is best. God provides the path for those who please Him.

Eternal Rewards: The Bible promises everlasting rewards for those who seek to please God. Matthew 25:21 records Jesus saying, "Well done, good and faithful servant! You have been faithful with a few things; I will entrust you with many things. Come and share your master's happiness!" Paul reminded the believers at Colossae, "Whatever you do, work at it with all your heart, as working for the Lord, not for me, since you know that you will receive an inheritance from the Lord as a reward." (Colossians 3:23-24)

Protection and Provision: God promises to protect and provide for those who seek to please Him. Psalm 34:9-10 states, "Fear the Lord, you his holy people, for those who fear him lack nothing. The lions may grow weak and hungry, but those who seek the Lord lack no good thing."

Strength and Support: Pleasing God guarantees His strength and support in times of need. Isaiah 40:31 states, "But those who hope in the Lord will renew their strength. They will soar on wings like eagles; they will run and not grow weary, they will walk and not be faint."

Healthy Relationships: Pleasing God can lead to healthier and more harmonious relationships with others. Adhering to God's principles of love, kindness, and forgiveness often improves our interactions with those around us. God consistently promotes favor in the relationships of those who please Him.

A Clear Conscience: Living in a way that pleases God helps keep a clear conscience, free from guilt and shame. Acts 24:16 emphasizes this: "So I strive always to keep my conscience clear before God and man." Our conscience won't be misled by the enemy's taunt that God no longer loves us. When our conscience is clear, we stop assuming that every crisis is a punishment from the Lord.

The benefits of pleasing the Lord include both temporary and eternal rewards, along with improvements in one's spiritual life, relationships, and overall well-being. We seek these qualities as we pursue the life we've always desired. It is a mistake to think that these blessings are available to those whose lives do not please the Lord. These traits and blessings can only be achieved by following the right path.

Scripture offers guidance on living according to God's will. Finding this path can be difficult when we are unsure about what the Bible teaches about God, Christianity, and how to please Him. Often, the road is obscured by myths that have distorted the message of Scripture.

Reflect & Respond

As you finish this chapter, take a few quiet moments to reflect on what God might be speaking to your heart. These questions help you remember key truths, deepen your understanding, challenge your assumptions, and motivate you to action. Whether you're working through them alone or with a group, invite the Holy Spirit to guide your thoughts, encourage honest conversations, and reveal the next step in your walk with Christ. Let this be not just a review but a response of faith, obedience, and transformation.

1. According to A.W. Tozer and the teachings in this chapter, how is true faith connected to pleasing God, and what does this reveal about the nature of authentic Christian living?

2. How does this chapter distinguish between God's unconditional love and His pleasure in our lives, and why is understanding that difference vital for spiritual growth?

3. In what ways has the American Dream been conflated with God's plan for our lives, and how does this misunderstanding impact our values, priorities, and pursuit of God's will?

4. List and reflect on at least four areas that show a genuine desire to please God. In which areas do you feel the strongest, and where do you need the most growth, and why?

5. What are three specific biblical rewards associated with pleasing God, and how does pursuing His pleasure influence your decision-making and spiritual growth? (Include Scripture references if possible.)

CHAPTER TWO

THE MYTHS WE BELIEVE

*As I urged you when I went into Macedonia,
stay there in Ephesus so that you may command certain
men not to teach false doctrines any longer nor to devote
themselves to myths and endless genealogies. These promote
controversies rather than God's work—which is by faith.
(1 Timothy 1:3–4)*

Scripture reminds us that not everyone pleases the Lord. Pleasing the Lord depends on walking the right path.

*This is what the Lord says: 'Stand at the crossroads and look; ask for the ancient paths, ask where the good way is, and walk in it, and you will find rest for your souls.'
(Jeremiah 6:16)*

Jeremiah reminds us that a righteous path exists in ancient traditions, while Jesus highlights how hard it is to find it.

Enter through the narrow gate. For wide is the gate and broad is the road that leads to destruction, and many enter through it. But small is the gate and narrow the road that leads to life, and only a few find it. (Matthew 7:13-14)

Later, Jesus reminds his disciples that he is "the way, the truth, and the life. No one comes to the Father except through me" (John 14:6). Christianity is often rejected because of its exclusive claim to be the only path to the true God. Any effort to please God begins with discovering this pathway. Jesus taught that following him on this path requires "taking up the cross" and losing one's life (Matthew 10:38-39). True Christianity was never meant to be easy.

If the path to pleasing the Lord is clear in Scripture, why do so many believers struggle to find it? Over fifty years in ministry, I have spoken with many believers trying to please God with their lives. Yet, only a few understand the spiritual habits necessary to bring a smile to God's face. We become so focused on doing that we forget to simply be. We mistakenly believe that knowing Scripture and praying are enough. In a survey I conducted while in seminary, I asked students, "How would I know you knew God?" The majority equated knowing the Bible and its teachings with proof of knowing God. However, in 1 John, we read, "Whoever does not love does not know God, because God is love" (1 John 4:8). Knowing the Word should lead to living it out in practical and visible ways. We can please God only by acting on His Word.

> *To the man who pleases him, God gives wisdom, knowledge and happiness, but to the sinner he gives the task of gathering and storing up wealth to hand it over to the one who pleases God. This too is meaningless, a chasing after the wind. (Ecclesiastes 2:26)*

Finding the Pathway through the Gospel

> *For this reason, since the day we heard about you, we have not stopped praying for you and asking God to fill you with the knowledge of his will through all spiritual wisdom and understanding. And we pray this in order that you may live a life worthy of the Lord and may please him in every way.... (Colossians 1:9-10)*

What had Paul heard about them? Paul writes from prison, surrounded by friends. One of these friends is Epaphras, who brings the exciting news that the gospel of Jesus Christ has not only changed the lives of the people in Colossae but has also affected the surrounding area. The gospel's power continues to transform lives. Paul had heard rumors, but Epaphras's message confirmed the authenticity of what he had heard.

> *All over the world this gospel is bearing fruit and growing, just as it has been doing among you since the day you heard it and understood God's grace in all its truth. You learned it from Epaphras, our dear fellow servant, who is a faithful minister of Christ on our behalf, and who also told us of your love in the Spirit. (Colossians 1:6-8)*

The journey starts with accepting the Gospel of Jesus Christ. No one can follow the path to please God without recognizing who Jesus is and what He has done. It took me years to fully understand and accept this truth in my life.

This book has held a special place in my heart for many years. Like many believers, my journey with the Lord started with more questions than answers after accepting the gospel. What does it take to please God? What does God expect from us? Is it truly possible to please God? God continually reveals His desires for His children. Throughout history, Israel has often forgotten the simplicity of His plea. When we stray from His path and God tries to reach out to us, our response, much like Israel's, can be sarcastic.

> *With what shall I come before the Lord and bow down before the exalted God? Shall I come before him with burnt offerings, with calves a year old? Will the Lord be pleased with thousands of rams, with ten thousand rivers of oil? Shall I offer my firstborn for my transgression, the fruit of my body for the sin of my soul? He has showed you, O man, what is good. And what does the Lord require of you? To act justly and to love mercy and to walk humbly with your God. (Micah 6:6–8)*

What is the purpose of the Christian life? What does a humble walk with the Lord look like? Over the past fifty years of ministry, I have heard nearly every answer common among believers. Some say it is about "bearing fruit" in our lives. By "fruit," they mean "souls." Those who hold this view believe that the measure of acceptance is witnessing to the lost, hoping that some will accept Jesus as fruit. Others think that living according to the Ten Commandments is the goal. Some suggest that religious participation is key. "I go to church, tithe, and teach a class to be okay with God," some insist. Many of our answers come from a series of misconceptions. Embracing the gospel begins with understanding it. Our understanding starts by discarding common myths about God and His gospel.

Myth: Most know who God is.

Paul taught that God is the God of hope. Many of us see God as an angry deity with unreasonable expectations. I encountered this view among Jewish survivors of the Holocaust. After graduating from college, I started my first job as a medical technologist in a small clinical lab. I was the only Gentile there; everyone else in the lab was a Jewish survivor of the Holocaust. As a Christian, I naively believed that being Jewish meant I had a shared connection with them. I thought we both worshiped the same God.

Suggesting they were God's people created ongoing conflict during my years there. The Holocaust demonstrated that God, if He existed, was a bully and a sadist. I had no leverage in this situation. I was an upper-middle-class white kid (Gentile) who had never faced any trouble. After the first blow-up, we agreed to avoid discussing anything related to God again. I complied until the Six-Day War erupted in Israel.

On the first day of the war, I arrived at the lab to find television sets in several rooms broadcasting news of the conflict. As I powered up the lab equipment, I casually remarked, "I think Israel will win the war; the Jews are God's people." Several people threatened to start their own war with me if I didn't stop "that nonsense." Six days later, the war ended with Israel as the victor. Things changed.

We began discussing the Old Testament and its stories about the history of God's people. I encouraged them to find a Hebrew Bible and read it themselves. Over the next few months, I became the lab's Gentile "rabbi." When I left the lab to pursue my graduate studies, their view of God shifted from hostile denial to cautious curiosity.

When we read Paul's exhortation to the Romans, "May the God of hope fill you..." The promise depends on how well we understand who God truly is. One of the biggest myths many of us believe is seeing God in the wrong light, much like my Jewish lab family. I believe the enemy works tirelessly to persuade us that God is responsible for all the bad in our lives.

We see examples of this in nearly every tragedy. Fred (not his real name) sat in my office, crying into a box of Kleenex. The day before, Fred had found a note from his wife, Cynthia (not her real name), on the kitchen table. The note revealed that she was in love with her boss and was leaving Fred for him.

Sitting with Fred, my heart ached for both of them. Fred asked, "Why would God do this to me?"

"God didn't do this, Fred; your wife did it," I said.

I wanted Fred to understand that God is not a bully. He does not force us to be faithful when we choose not to be. We often wonder why, if God is all-powerful, He doesn't prevent the Cynthias in our lives from being unfaithful. Fred and my Jewish friends did not see God as the "God of hope." In their misunderstanding, they attributed all their hurt to Him. We will never find peace and hope until we realize that our God is a God of hope.

Myth: If God loved us, he would rescue us from suffering.

Sometimes, we feel anger toward God because He isn't as decisive as we want. We question why an all-powerful God seems so powerless in some situations. This feeling stems from our belief that God will save us from all pain and suffering. If God truly cared, He would protect us from danger. Linda believed this myth. While sitting in my office, she expressed concern, reflecting her belief that if God truly loved us, He would prevent us from eternal separation.

"Do you believe in hell?"

I was taken aback by the question. I had recently officiated at her brother's funeral, who had died from a drug overdose. They had been very close, and his death affected her in ways she hadn't expected.

"Yes, I believe hell exists. Why?"

"Why would God send people to hell if He is a loving God?" she pressed. "Do you like the idea of hell?" she asked, fiddling with the tear-soaked Kleenex in her hand.

Linda lived near a park. For a few years, she sometimes saw a teenager camping there. Several times, she approached him to see if he needed anything, and sometimes she brought him food. She bought him a coat during his first winter and later gave him a blanket. She spent hours trying to find help for him. Several times a year, the police raided his camp and removed him, but since he was an emancipated minor, he always returned to the park. Linda felt burdened for him but also helpless. I listened to her concerns several times.

Linda, can I ask you something? Imagine tonight, when you drive past the park, you stop and offer help to the young man you mentioned to me. You say to him, 'I live on the edge of the park. I have a four-bedroom house, and I live alone. I want to offer you free room and board in my home. I'm willing to assist with job training or education so you can live independently. Would you be willing to stay in my house – it wouldn't cost you anything?' After you finish your generous offer, he gives you the finger and tells you to leave him alone. What would you do?

I'd probably get in my car and leave him be.

"Why would you do that? You care about him; wouldn't you pressure him to accept your offer because you care?" I asked.

"Well, no, that wouldn't be appropriate."

"Why not? You care about him!"

"If he rejects my offer, it wouldn't be right to force him to accept it. That isn't a socially acceptable way to behave."

"Why do you think God should force His will and love on everyone who rejects His offer to love and care for them?"

Later in the book, we will explore God's will more thoroughly. Scripture states that God desires all people to be saved, but most will not be. He has the power to save everyone but will only save those who choose to leave the park. We are part of a divine partnership with God. Some parts of His will require our cooperation to come to pass. It is wrong to blame God for not being the bully we sometimes accuse Him of being. Sometimes, we believe Him to be who He says He is, but we don't fully trust Him.

Myth: We all trust God.

Believing he is the God of hope is simply the first step in learning how to please him. (Anonymous)

And without faith it is impossible to please God, because anyone who comes to him must believe that he exists and that he rewards those who earnestly seek him.
(Hebrews 11:6)

I recall a seminary lecture where the professor, while discussing the attributes of God, drew a line on the whiteboard that encircled the classroom. One continuous line, interrupted only at the ends of each board. When he finished, he said,

"The line symbolizes God's presence and omnipotence throughout eternity." Then he walked over to a section of the line and drew a dot on it.

"This dot," he said, "represents your life. Explain to me how it is possible to trust God for his presence and control throughout all eternity," as his hand pointed around the room, "but not trust him with our checkbook, possessions, job, house, and everything else in our lives?"

Faith can be a tricky concept. It's one thing to believe that parachutes work; it's quite another to strap one on and jump out of an airplane. It's easier to trust God for all eternity and our salvation than to trust Him to meet our daily needs. Paul reminds us that the benefits of committing to that kind of faith —putting on the parachute and jumping—are rewarded with joy, peace, and hope (Romans 15:13). Hope only arises after we trust that God is trustworthy. Sometimes, another myth hinders our trust.

Myth: Contentment always comes with salvation.

I rejoice greatly in the Lord that at last you have renewed your concern for me. Indeed, you have been concerned, but you had no opportunity to show it. I am not saying this because I am in need, for I have learned to be content whatever the circumstances. I know what it is to be in need, and I know what it is to have plenty. I have learned the secret of being content in any and every situation, whether well fed or hungry, whether living in plenty or in want. I can do everything through him who gives me strength. (Philippians 4:10-13)

Embracing the gospel requires complete trust in God. Ironically, we trust God for our salvation but hesitate to rely on Him for our daily needs. Paul reminded the church in Philippi that being content is a secret—one that can be found and learned. One of the biggest misconceptions about God comes from blending biblical and cultural beliefs. The most significant dilution for American believers is merging the Bible with American culture. This dilution acts as a filter. Many American Christians have developed an unhealthy habit of viewing the world through this lens. Our culture suggests we can achieve the American Dream with enough time, resources, personal effort, and luck. This dream includes independence, extra leisure time, a beautiful home in a pleasant neighborhood, and financial freedom. We value our liberty and our right to pursue happiness. Although we may not define it clearly, happiness remains our goal. We must ask ourselves, "Is the American Dream a by-product of embracing the gospel of Jesus Christ?" Is happiness the same as contentment?

Paul suggests that the primary concern for believers is not happiness, but contentment. I've always found Paul's message to the Philippian church powerful. Contentment is a secret that must be learned before it can be genuinely felt. The American way often stresses working harder to reach the American

Dream. God's way calls us to depend on Him for everything and to develop contentment, whether we are rich or poor. Paul finds the answer through trust and the strength that comes from God. If we want to please God, our faith in Him must be steady. We should be believers who view the world and culture through the lens of our understanding of Him and His Word. We are believers first, Americans second. But being American or following a culture isn't the only challenge believers face when trusting God for everything.

Myth: We all understand the Gospel.

I am astonished that you are so quickly deserting the one who called you by the grace of Christ and are turning to a different gospel— which is really no gospel at all. Evidently some people are throwing you into confusion and are trying to pervert the gospel of Christ. (Galatians 1:6-7)

Many of us are uncertain about what the gospel truly is. Unknowingly, the Galatian believers shifted the focus of the gospel from faith in Christ alone to faith mixed with works. Paul warns that the gospel ceases to be the gospel once it is combined with any other teachings. The Galatian church taught that salvation comes through faith in Jesus, but they also believed maintaining salvation required obedience to the law. Without realizing it, they added performance into the equation. Surveys show that many modern Christians follow the same heresy as the Galatians.

One of the challenges of living the Christian life is that progress can sometimes be difficult to measure. We all want to know whether we are meeting God's expectations. We understand that He will not be pleased unless we pass His tests. Church attendance, time spent reading the Bible, abstaining from sinful acts, and giving money are all easier to measure than accurately assessing qualities like love, trust, or maturity. These are abstract concepts that are hard to quantify. Like many of us, the Galatian believers struggled with the question, "How do I know if God is pleased with me?" Their solution was to introduce some measurements, such as the law. We must "grow up" in our faith because everything God expects from us depends on our maturity to understand the goal. God's aim is for us to become more like Jesus each day. When we add the law or a fixed set of rules to the Christian life, we dilute the message and make it so confusing that we miss the true goal. We miss out on pleasing the Lord. A final distortion of the truth is highlighted in Hebrews.

> We have much to say about this, but it is hard to explain because you are slow to learn. In fact, though by this time you ought to be teachers, you need someone to teach you the elementary truths of God's word all over again. You need milk, not solid food! Anyone who lives on milk, being still an infant, is not acquainted with the teaching about righteousness. But solid food is for the mature, who by constant use have trained themselves to distinguish good from evil. Therefore let us leave the elementary teachings about Christ and go on to maturity, not laying again the foundation of repentance from acts that lead to death, and of faith in God, instruction about baptisms, the laying on of hands, the resurrection of the dead, and eternal judgment. (Hebrews 5:11– 6:2)

The author of Hebrews addresses Christian Jews, expressing concern that by the time he wrote, they should have matured in their Christian faith enough to teach others about living as mature Christians. Instead, he encourages them to revisit the basics and pursue spiritual growth. What had they done? Rather than fully abandoning Judaism for their new faith in Jesus, they combined Christianity with their existing Judaism. Having grown up with formal Judaism, complete with its religious rules and rituals, this mixture diluted their experience, preventing them from fully enjoying the joys and growth that come only through Jesus. Strangely, this situation reflects that of many average American Christians.

Many have added church activities to an already busy

schedule. Most women in the church where I serve work outside the home out of necessity. Sociologically, this reality has significantly impacted our culture. Tasks that were once spread throughout the week are now often pushed to the weekend. With both parents working, a new category called Latchkey Kids has emerged to describe the growing number of children who come home from school long before a parent arrives. Summers have become a challenge for these children because most parents don't get the summer off from work. As a result, they need to find someone to care for their kids. When the weekend arrives, we clean the house, wash clothes, shop for groceries, participate in Little League activities, connect with friends, mow the lawn, wash the car, catch up on family relationships, and attend church. Being involved with other believers adds to an already full schedule. The demands of life can dilute our relationship with the Lord, robbing us of the opportunity to learn contentment and experience the growth and maturity needed to please Him. Ironically, God has always given us the time to accomplish His will. Our busyness often prevents us from truly pleasing Him.

The enemy attempts to weaken our faith through distractions. One of his most effective tactics is convincing us that our main goal should be to understand the Bible.

Myth: Working on my salvation is legalism.

Therefore, my dear friends, as you have always obeyed—not only in my presence, but now much more in my absence—continue to work out your salvation with fear and trembling, for it is God who works in you to will and to act according to his good purpose. (Philippians 2:12-13)

Philippians 2:12-13 teaches that the Christian life requires both human effort and divine strength. We should live thoughtfully and purposefully in obedience to God, trusting that He empowers our growth in both desire and action. This leads us to a life that pleases Him and accomplishes His purpose. It is not legalistic to believe that God expects us to be involved in our salvation.

Legalism claims that works save us. Here, Paul reminds us that we are in a divine partnership with God. God saved us from the penalty of sin; He energizes us to live victoriously over the power of sin; and He will, in the future, remove us from the presence of sin. Living passively while battling sin is a mistake. God will not grant us success without effort or obedience on our part. In his brief letter, Jude reminds us that we must actively work on building ourselves up.

> But you, dear friends, build yourselves up in your most holy faith and pray in the Holy Spirit. Keep yourselves in God's love as you wait for the mercy of our Lord Jesus Christ to bring you to eternal life. (Jude 20–21)

Paul reminds Timothy that even when we have failed, hope remains — as long as we're willing to take action.

> In a large house there are articles not only of gold and silver, but also of wood and clay; some are for noble purposes and some for ignoble. If a man cleanses himself from the latter, he will be an instrument for noble purposes, made holy, useful to the Master and prepared to do any good work. (2 Timothy 2:20-21)

Believing this myth is a costly mistake. It encourages those who neglect to develop habits that refresh the mind and honor God. Too often, we pray and memorize scripture without actively practicing our salvation. This mindset makes it much easier to accept the next myth.

Myth: Knowing the Bible is the goal.

I grew up in a church that highly valued the Bible. Maturity and acceptance were judged by how well someone understood the Word. As a teenager, I remember going to youth group and participating in a "Bible Drill." A verse would be announced, and we would all race to find it first. I never invited anyone to the youth group. Our family felt responsible for the boy living across the street. I recall my mom encouraging me to invite him to join our youth group, but I never did. I pictured him taking part in a Bible Drill.

I was raised in a faith community that taught me the Bible was God's inerrant and infallible Word. I am very grateful for having learned the Word. However, it came with some unintended consequences. We distanced ourselves from other believers who didn't share our views about the Bible, and we eventually ended up worshiping the book. As I grew into adulthood, I lived within a framework filled with myths and misconceptions. Many of us forgot that Christianity is a relationship, not a religion. Instead, we turned it into a religion. Looking back on my early years, I see we resembled the Church of Galatia.

Over more than twenty years in my church, we moved from being connected with hundreds of other churches to ultimately standing alone. We felt isolated! We mistakenly believed the Bible taught us to separate from other believers who didn't interpret every passage the same way we did. Looking back, I see we prioritized indoctrination over education. I grew up thinking that God was pleased with how we approached His Word. I also felt that His approval of me depended on my ability to "rightly divide the Word." I was a Pharisee without even realizing it.

It is a mistake to make understanding the Bible our primary goal in life. Knowing the Bible is just the first step in pleasing the Lord. A proper understanding of the Bible should transform our behavior and enable us to cultivate a personal relationship with the triune God. Embracing the gospel fosters a daily desire for change and to become more like Jesus. As we grow and change, we see that knowing Him becomes more important than just learning about Him.

Grace and peace be yours in abundance through the knowledge of God and of Jesus our Lord. (2 Peter 1:2)

Growing up, I understood that Peter taught, "You will discover grace and peace by knowing more about God and Jesus."

That thought inspired me to study Scripture more deeply. Later, I learned he said, "You will experience grace and peace as you develop a personal, intimate relationship with God and His Son." The idea of knowledge is clear in the question, "How well do you know God?" My understanding shifted from merely knowing the Bible to knowing its Author. I reflect on those years in church with mixed emotions. At the age of seven, I accepted Jesus as my Savior, and I still vividly remember that event. Yet, for many years, I regarded the Bible as a textbook to master. The more I learned about it, the more I came to believe that God was pleased with me. When I was twenty, I realized that, although I knew the Bible well, some parts of my life needed to change. Without realizing it, I had fallen victim to our next myth: we refuse to change.

Myth: Growth automatically begins at salvation.

Our lives are changed by those who love us and those who refuse to.
John Powell

In my late twenties, I read John Powell's books multiple times. Despite growing up in a loving Christian home, I felt a deep emptiness. I was at odds with everyone around me. I could explain what the Bible and many philosophers say about love, but my understanding of the topic hadn't changed how I behaved. Love was still a concept to be analyzed and dissected. It was something to understand intellectually rather than a behavior to imitate, reflecting the invisible God. God used a casual conversation while I was working in healthcare to start transforming my loveless life.

My boss was aware I was a seminary student. As a clinical laboratory scientist working the evening shift, I could study in my office as long as I completed all my tasks. One evening, I was preparing for a Hebrew exam. Hebrew texts, theology notes, and my Bible were spread across my desk. A coworker entered my office and sink into one of the chairs.

"You don't like me, do you?" he asked.

Before I could respond, he said, "Aren't you a seminary student? . . . A seminary student should be loving, but I don't see much of that in your life."

Before I could reply, he turned and left my office. At first, I felt angry; he had no right to say that to me. Later, during a coffee break with a nurse who had become a close friend, I told her about the incident. She listened quietly.

"Why do you think he would say something like that?" she asked.

The question hung in the air like a coming storm cloud.

"Do you think I'm unloving?" I asked honestly.

The cloud grew larger.

"You are a good person with a lot of knowledge and are rarely wrong. You're usually accurate but often lack kindness or empathy toward others who disagree."

Suddenly, thunder rumbled and lightning flashed. I realized she was right. Amid my thoughts, my pager buzzed. A serious accident had occurred, and the emergency room needed lab work for several patients. I don't remember much of the evening, but I recall getting into my car and feeling exhausted. As I drove out of the parking lot, I started to cry. God used those conversations that night to help me face the truth that I wasn't a loving person. I hadn't fully embraced the gospel. I saw accepting Christ as just joining His family rather than a life shaped by His image. That night marked the beginning of a journey I am still on. My journey started with the realization that love is something learned. I hadn't become loving overnight. Like any skill, I needed to develop new behaviors. You never fully arrive, but you get closer. My first step in learning to love was to repent.

Repentance originates from the Greek word "metanoia." It encompasses two aspects: a change of mind and a commitment to pursue a new direction. It involves leaving something behind to embrace something new. Paul's concern with the Church in Galatia was not about legalism. Legalism claims that God accepts a person who follows the rules of Scripture (the law). Very few believe this. While the believers in Galatia did not accept legalism, they thought that although Christ had paid the price for their sins, they could maintain a good standing by following rules and laws. Looking back, I realize I once believed the same thing. As a result, knowing the Bible accurately felt essential for my acceptance by God. I demonstrated my knowledge of Him by showing others how well I understood the Scriptures. J. I. Packer reminds us in his book, "Knowing God," that most of us have extensive knowledge about God, but few know Him personally. Our relationship, or lack thereof, with God is revealed not by what we know, but by how we love.

> *Dear friends, let us love one another, for love comes from God. Everyone who loves has been born of God and knows God. Whoever does not love does not know God, because God is love. (1 John 4:7–8)*

Embracing the gospel means learning to love, which requires me to change my worldview. I grew up believing my role was to be right. I needed to defend the Bible, which involved understanding its teachings and rules. I developed a critical mindset, viewing everyone as an enemy unless they met my standards of Christianity. They were viewed with suspicion if they used the wrong version, dressed inappropriately, attended the wrong church, or participated in secular community events; the list went on and on.

Some of us, like my former self, resist change. Those around us often stop urging us because they believe we will eventually outgrow it. Growing and changing are two different ideas. Change involves behaviors that need immediate attention. Our lives could be deeply affected if we don't address them right away.

On the other hand, growth is a long-term process as God works to refine who we are and shape us into the image of Jesus. I have met men who have spent their lives consumed by anger. People never confronted them about their issues.

Everyone around them hoped they would outgrow their rage. Instead, they went to their graves as angry men. They needed to be challenged about change. We need someone to point out our shortcomings and hold us accountable for our problems. Only after we change can we begin to mature, assuming we are willing to do so.

Myth: It's OK to embrace the gospel without being fruitful.

This is the meaning of the parable: The seed is the word of God. Those along the path are the ones who hear, and then the devil comes and takes away the word from their hearts, so that they may not believe and be saved. Those on the rock are the ones who receive the word with joy when they hear it, but they have no root. They believe for a while, but in the time of testing they fall away. The seed that fell among thorns stands for those who hear, but as they go on their way they are choked by life's worries, riches and pleasures, and they do not mature. But the seed on good soil stands for those with a noble and good heart, who hear the word, retain it, and by persevering produce a crop. (Luke 8:11-15)

Jesus' parable has always challenged me. Questions about pleasing God can only be answered by understanding and applying Scripture to our lives. Jesus implies that this requires spiritual maturity. Mature individuals are fruitful, and fruitful individuals please God. The parable suggests that 75% of the seeds sown did not produce any fruit.

Many of us are too immature to grasp the deeper truths of pleasing God. Our immaturity causes us to focus on "life's worries, riches, and pleasures." Paul expresses his frustration with the church in Corinth when he writes:

Brothers, I could not address you as spiritual but as worldly, mere infants in Christ. (1 Corinthians 3:1)

As we have already seen, the author of Hebrews shared a similar concern. When describing Melchizedek, he pauses, acknowledging that his readers are not mature enough to understand this subject in more detail (Hebrews 5:11-14). Like the recipients of the letter to the Hebrews, the church is full of immature believers who, because of their immaturity, cannot grasp or apply the deeper truths of Scripture. Several key shifts indicate the transition from immaturity to maturity. The areas listed below highlight immaturity and hinder our growth.

- Growth is a journey from dependence to independence and then to interdependence. The immature depend on others for their needs or become so independent that they isolate themselves socially. One of the first signs of maturity is recognizing our interdependence. Paul's exhortations about the importance of "one another" are missed by the immature. Our relationships with others hold lasting value.

- Adolescents, on their path from immaturity to maturity, transition from egocentrism to other-centrism. Immaturity claims, "It's all about me." The challenge of immaturity occurs when attention shifts from oneself to others. Their work, relationships, entertainment, and daily routines focus on personal gain. However, as maturity develops, considering others becomes essential, giving the Bible a deeper significance.

- As individuals mature, they transition from passivity to proactivity. Individuals who lack maturity often expect to be taken care of and feel entitled. Many immature men wait passively beside their wives, relying on them to figure things out before being prompted to take the initiative and do what mature men do independently. Those who are mature take a proactive approach. Living the Christian life demands proactivity. God's children are not called to live lives of passivity. Pleasing the Lord and resembling Jesus require intentional living.

- The process of maturity involves moving from a

pleasure-focused mindset to one centered on purpose. For teenagers, their comfort zone is considered a sacred space. They are unable to see that growth and maturity arise from tension and discomfort. They remain unaware of how purpose and goals contribute to growth and well-being.

- Growing up means moving from just learning to applying what we know. It's not about how much a person knows; the true measure of success and maturity is using that knowledge in practice. The immature can tell you what needs to be done, but only the mature take action.

When we refuse to mature and be fruitful, we limit our ability to please the Lord. Our immaturity leads us to seek approval from others and conform to their cultural norms.

Myth: We can simultaneously embrace the gospel and cultural norms.

We live in a culture that is constantly changing. One major shift is the decreasing acceptance of absolutes. As society evolves, the truth of the Bible remains unchanged. However, some people soften the Bible's message to make Christianity more appealing to the general public. In today's society, claiming that Jesus is the only way to God can seem rigid and harsh. I was shocked when I heard a church member pray, "Oh God, Jehovah, Allah, be with us today..." The Bible teaches that there is only one God—Jehovah. Allah is not another name for God. This misguided prayer illustrates how some people succumb to cultural pressure out of fear that others might be offended by the truth of Scripture. Just as always, Scripture stands as a counterculture to any human-made culture without God.

As I transitioned from being a Pharisee to a loving believer, my attitude toward those who don't meet the biblical standard of living reflected one of the most meaningful changes in my life. I shifted from being an angry, self-righteous Pharisee to embodying an expression of God's love for people. God continues to love a world filled with individuals who choose to hate Him and His children. Sometimes, we may be the only reflection of God that others will see. This is the message of John.

> *Dear friends, since God so loved us, we also ought to love one another. No one has ever seen God; but if we love one another, God lives in us and his love is made complete in us. (1 John 4:11-12)*

The Bible should define who we are, not culture. Still, we should live and love in a way that shows loving others is more important than being right. This is tough in a culture that often resists disagreement. We are called to embody a counterculture that no one can fully accept or live without embracing the gospel of Jesus Christ. We will never please God through rude behavior or by watering down the difficult message of Scripture. The Holy Spirit will use Scripture's challenging message to convict others of their need for a Savior. We are ambassadors of God's love.

Myth: Everyone knows what the term 'Christian' means.

A few years ago, a pastor friend visited a mosque in Cairo, Egypt, and sat with a group of men. He sat there in quiet meditation for nearly an hour until the man next to him turned and asked if he was a follower of Muhammad.

"No, I follow Jesus," he said.

The man smiled and greeted him at the mosque.

Since then, he has had several opportunities to meet and spend time with his new friend. When I heard this story, I asked him why he didn't identify as a Christian.

"I grew up in a culture," he responded, "that associates Christianity with the Crusades and open hostility toward Islam. For many Muslims, the term 'Christian' carries a negative connotation. They see Christianity not only as a long-standing adversary but also as a symbol of decadence and arrogance. However, they acknowledge Jesus as a prophet. If they saw me as a disciple of Jesus, they would likely not question my presence."

A week later, I met a young man who represented his country at OPEC. He believed he was the only Christian in his office and described himself as a "Follower of Jesus." This was the second time that week I heard the term "Follower of Jesus" instead of "Christian." Again, I asked why he chose that word and if he felt embarrassed about being linked to Christianity. His answer surprised me.

He explained that most OPEC members he worked with had never been to the United States. The media and their Islamic perspective on how the world and relationships work shape their views of America. The United States is often shown in the press as a country filled with pornography, widespread drug use, rebellion, and political scandals. Although a free press is one of the most important parts of our free society, this freedom can harm our image worldwide. With the rise of social media today, the world is more aware of all our failures. Since good news isn't profitable, the positive stories of our compassion and morality are rarely shared. "When someone identifies as a Christian," he said, "they are associated with everything wrong in America."

The term "Christian" has become less respected, even in the United States. Unsurprisingly, many Christians share some of the same Islamic views about America. The American Christian notices the surrounding decadence and greed. Like Lot, they should be upset by the tendency to accept all ungodly behavior as normal. Some long for the nation to return to a time when most citizens clearly understood what was right and wrong.

The nuances of this world system are gradually infiltrating a significant portion of the Christian population in America. We are becoming so similar to the world that we have slipped into a form of functional atheism. A functional atheist is someone who claims to believe in God and His redemptive plan but lives from Monday to Saturday as if God doesn't exist. They also contribute to the misunderstanding of Christianity, filling some of the best churches in America. Many of them are good people who confuse religion with a real relationship.

Christianity has never just been a religion or a political party;

it has always been about a relationship with a Savior who loves us and paid the price for our sins. Although most churches in our country affirm this belief, they often lose sight of God's purpose for the church and the believer. We can truly become Christians only when we re-embrace the gospel and rediscover this purpose. When we collectively become genuine Christians, God will work through us to transform the hearts of a nation. This transformation happens only after fully embracing the gospel and God's will for our lives.

Reflect & Respond

As you finish this chapter, take a few quiet moments to reflect on what God might be speaking to your heart. These questions help you remember key truths, deepen your understanding, challenge your assumptions, and motivate you to action. Whether you're working through them alone or with a group, invite the Holy Spirit to guide your thoughts, encourage honest conversations, and reveal the next step in your walk with Christ. Let this be not just a review but a response of faith, obedience, and transformation.

1. *Why did Jesus describe the gate and the road that lead to life as "narrow," and how does this challenge common assumptions about Christian life?*

2. *According to the writer of Hebrews, why were Jewish believers criticized for needing milk instead of solid food? What does this reveal about the importance of applying biblical truth?*

3. *In what ways might American culture, which emphasizes happiness and self-fulfillment, undermine biblical faith and distort our understanding of true contentment?*

4. *How does the myth that "knowing the Bible is the goal" reflect the mindset of the Pharisees, and what dangers arise from approaching Scripture this way?*

5. *What common myths or misconceptions about God have you*

encountered or believed, and how has this chapter challenged or corrected those beliefs? Can you identify areas where these misconceptions have influenced your relationship with God?

CHAPTER THREE

KNOWING GOD'S WILL

True faith rests in the will of God.
Our greatest pleasure should be to please Him.
A. W. Tozer

Paul reminds us that salvation's power is found in the gospel. Because of this, he is not ashamed of it (Romans 1:16-17). He reaffirms this truth by telling the Colossian believers, "All over the world, this gospel is bearing fruit and growing, just as it has been doing among you since the day you heard it and understood God's grace in all its truth" (Colossians 1:6). Its transformative power is evident in your lives, which is truly awe-inspiring. Paul emphasizes the impact of the gospel in his letter to the Ephesian church.

> *For you were once darkness, but now you are light in the Lord. Live as children of light (for the fruit of the light consists in all goodness, righteousness and truth) and find out what pleases the Lord. (Ephesians 5:8-10)*

The gospel changes lives and leads us on a new journey. Phillip E. Johnson experienced this powerful transformation from darkness to light. Born in 1940, he graduated from Harvard University and the University of Chicago with a law degree by age 25. After graduation, he worked as a clerk for Chief Justice Earl Warren at the U.S. Supreme Court. He later moved to California with his second wife and child to teach at the University of California, Berkeley School of Law. During the summer, his 7-year-old daughter attended vacation Bible school at a local church. One Friday night, after the vacation Bible school, parents were invited to a program celebrating its completion. It was there that he heard the gospel for the first time. It may be hard to believe, but he later admitted during a meeting with local pastors that he had never heard the gospel before that day. His encounter with Jesus changed his life and profoundly impacted the world. He became a leading advocate for creationism and helped popularize the idea of Intelligent Design as an alternative to evolution.

Can you believe it? He had never heard the gospel before! God used several hundred people to share a clear message about His love for Phillip, which changed his life forever. That night, a miracle happened, transforming his life from darkness into light. When we think of a miracle, we often imagine God healing cancer or raising the dead. However, the greatest miracle is when someone is brought from darkness into light. You cannot begin the Christian life without experiencing this miracle. Going through this miracle lays the foundation for pleasing God.

Many confuse being religious with being a Christian. Studies show that most Americans "believe" in God. When we look at this group, we find that while they are religious, many still live in darkness. The only way to be a Christian is to believe the good news (the gospel) that Jesus, God in human form, paid the price for our sins by dying on a Roman cross. The proof that God accepted Jesus' sacrifice on our behalf is found in His resurrection, as He was raised from death to life.

> He was delivered over to death for our sins and was raised to life for our justification. Therefore, since we have been justified through faith, we have peace with God through our Lord Jesus Christ, through whom we have gained access by faith into this grace in which we now stand. (Romans 4:25-5:2)

He "was raised to life for our justification," which means that he was resurrected because God accepted the sacrifice on our behalf. Each time someone accepts Jesus in connection with this sacrifice, they become a child of God. They are miraculously transferred from the kingdom of darkness to the kingdom of light. Peter reminded the early Christians that before this happened, they "were not a people, but now you are the people of God; once you had not received mercy, but now you have received mercy." (1 Peter 2:10)

> But you are a chosen people, a royal priesthood, a holy nation, a people belonging to God, that you may declare the praises of him who called you out of darkness into his wonderful light. (1 Peter 2:9)

Putting a smile on God's face begins with embracing the gospel. Embracing the gospel means releasing anything that blocks our transformation through the good news that God loves us and paid the price for our sins through His Son, allowing us to become His children. When we embrace the gospel, a new way to please God with the life we've always dreamed of opens up.

Where is the path leading?

Many believers who want to please God often seek guidance in Christian living. However, they should focus on building a relationship with the One who saved them. Following a set of rules is easier than developing a relationship, but the Christian life starts with that connection. This bond forms the foundation of God's will. We open the door to pleasing God by embracing His will for our lives; by following His will, we put ourselves on the path to our future. Paul understood this as he prayed for the people of Colossae.

> For this reason, since the day we heard about you, we have not stopped praying for you and asking God to fill you with the knowledge of his will through all spiritual wisdom and understanding. And we pray this in order that you may live a life worthy of the Lord and may please him in every way.... (Colossians 1:9-10)

Paul was deeply moved by the dramatic changes brought about by the gospel, which led him to pray constantly. He could have prayed about many things. The early church faced ongoing persecution; Rome despised them, and the Jewish religious leaders loathed them. The growing church faced increasing challenges that Paul might have prayed for. They had no permanent building or meeting place, relying on others to open their homes for gatherings. Paul doesn't seem troubled by these issues; he appears indifferent to financial concerns, the complexities of rapid church growth, and church governance. Upon hearing about the tremendous impact of the gospel, he centers his prayer on the primary goal—knowing and being guided by God's will, which leads to a life that pleases God.

Paul prays for the Colossian saints to be filled with the knowledge of God's will. The words he chooses are rich in nuanced meanings. It's important to pause here and explore the deeper significance of these words. What does he mean by using the term "filled"? Pleasing God cannot be achieved without a complete understanding of what it means to be filled. The term "filled" comes from the Greek word pleróō. Paul uses this word when talking about being filled with the Holy Spirit (Ephesians 5:18). The focus is on influence; we should let God's will and the Holy Spirit guide us, just as alcohol influences our bodies. Our resistance and hesitation to surrender control decreases. When this happens, we empower God's will and Spirit as He shapes our perceptions of life. We begin to show the fruit of the Spirit, revealing the way to please God. This filling leads us to a deeper understanding of God and His will. Paul's prayer is that every believer be so guided by God's will that it becomes the primary focus and goal in everything we do. Knowing God's will makes all the difference.

In Paul's letter to the Colossians, the word for knowledge in Colossians Chapter One is epígnōsis. This is one of three terms for knowledge used in Scripture. Each word conveys different levels of understanding while emphasizing specific aspects of knowledge.

The first of these three words translated as "knowledge" in the New Testament is oida, which means to have seen or perceived (thus, to know or have known). This represents the most basic form of knowledge and can describe either a relationship or an object. The second word for knowledge, ginosko, refers to the same body of knowledge but from the perspective of deeper understanding. We may know (oida) something without fully understanding it (ginosko). Often, this word is translated as "understanding." The third word translated as "knowledge" is epiginosko. This term signifies experiential knowledge and is the word chosen by the translators of the Septuagint to convey intimate knowledge. The New American Standard often translates this word as "true knowledge."

When used with objects, it refers to knowledge that guides our decisions. Having epiginosko knowledge lays the foundation for wise choices. A few examples will help us understand the profound differences between these words. When these words for knowledge are used with things, they describe knowledge that begins as superficial and gradually leads to wisdom.

I was a biochemistry minor in college. On the first day of biochemistry, Dr. Debay distributed the "Metabolic Pathways of the Human Body" chart to each student. The chart outlined the body's metabolic pathways and consisted of five pages, each measuring 36 by 48 inches, with formulae written in Times New Roman 12-point font.

"In your hands, you hold the metabolic pathways of the human body. You have six weeks to memorize this chart—all five pages. At the start of week seven, you will be asked to reproduce one or more of these pages," Dr. Debay stated casually and matter-of-factly.

I copied the chart onto 3x5 note cards in small sections to take home. It took several weeks to transfer the chart to those cards. Over the following weeks, I memorized the content. On

Monday morning of week 7, I successfully reproduced the first page of the chart during an exam. I demonstrated that I knew (oida) the chart. I understood some of it, but much of it remained unclear.

Throughout the rest of the year, Dr. Debay skillfully demonstrated God's creative genius in every part of the chart. A year later, I could recall most of the chart from memory and explain how the body produces energy, why some compounds generate more energy than others, how water and oxygen help the flow of life, and many other aspects of our metabolic pathways. I understood (ginosko) the chart. Later, while working in the clinical lab, I conducted tests to identify different components of the metabolic pathways as our doctors tried to pinpoint the source of a patient's pain. My understanding grew into epiginosko, and my knowledge guided which tests we chose. This process happens when we study scripture.

I remember studying 1 Corinthians 13:1-8 shortly after being confronted about my unloving behavior. Memorizing passages that define love was an excellent starting point for changing my actions. After a week, I had memorized the passage (oida). Next, I took out my interlinear Greek/English Bible and examined the words used to describe love. Before long, I understood what Paul was saying (ginosko). My background and past experiences helped me in this process. I have used this method many times before. The old me would have stopped here. In previous discussions, I could have lectured on the meaning of this passage. I often learned (ginosko) passages like this, thinking I knew them. At that point, I understood love in theory rather than in practice. In his letter to the Corinthians, Paul suggests that knowledge remaining at the ginosko stage leads to pride.

Now about food sacrificed to idols: We know that we all possess knowledge [ginosko]. Knowledge puffs up, but love builds up. (1 Corinthians 8:1)

I finished seminary, full of knowledge [ginosko], much of

which I had never truly experienced. My friend, who confronted me in my office, described me as someone "who knew a lot about love" but was unloving. I was "puffed up."

1 Corinthians 13 inspired me to list the measurable qualities of a loving person. For each quality, I identified a person or situation where I needed to practice it. There was a nurse at the hospital who was perceived by everyone as a bully. I set a goal to be kind and humble toward her. Over time, we became friends. Gradually, the Holy Spirit helped me apply this passage. My new experiential knowledge transformed me into a more loving person and revealed areas that needed attention.

This same progression from oida to epiginosko occurs in our relationships with others. I first met Dr. John Balyo during an interview at Western Baptist College (now Corban University). Several of us were asked to serve on the search committee for the college's next president. All I knew was that Dr. John Balyo held two doctorates: one in law and another in theology. During his visit, we spent several hours discussing the college and exploring the possibility of him accepting the position if it was offered. I was excited to finally meet him after hearing about him for years. Now, I knew him (oida). Several days later, he accepted the offer to serve as our president.

Over the next few years, John and I became close friends. As the Vice President of Student Services and Dean of Students, I served on Dr. Balyo's executive administrative council, which oversaw the daily operations of a small Christian liberal arts college each month. With every loss and victory, our bond as friends strengthened. I understood (ginosko) him and could predict his decisions on various issues. During his second year, John, Keith Cox (our Director of Development), and I began speaking at fundraising banquets, starting in Southern California and concluding in Northern Washington. We spoke at fifteen banquets each year for several years. Most of our travel was in the college car, and over time, we spent hundreds of hours packed into a vehicle driving to the next event. Our relationship grew to a point where we knew each other (epiginosko) as only family can.

You might wonder why I focus so much on the importance of true knowledge. Without it, we can't understand the link between God's will and how to please Him. Paul prays that when believers are filled with a sincere knowledge of God's will, they stand on the verge of living a life that is worthy of the Lord and fully pleasing to Him.

He guides our understanding of God's will with spiritual wisdom and insight. We question our decisions: are they moral and wise? You might wonder what steps we should take to find out. We are at a critical point. We can't just pray for God's will; it's unlikely to be shown in a dream or by a loud voice waking us up in the middle of the night. To understand God's will, we need to develop essential skills that He will use through the Holy Spirit to reveal Himself and His plans for our lives. Discovering God's will should be important to us, just as it was for Israel.

The next day, Moses sat to judge the people, and the people stood around Moses from morning till evening. When Moses' father-in-law saw all that he was doing for the people, he said, "What is this that you are doing for the people? Why do you sit alone, and all the people stand around you from morning till evening?" And Moses said to his father-in-law, "Because the people come to me to inquire of God; when they have a dispute, they come to me and I decide between one person and another, and I make them know the statutes of God and his laws. (Exodus 18:13-16)

For thousands of years, God's people have sought His will. Paul reminded the believers in Ephesus to be wise and seek God's will. Our desire to please God involves understanding His purpose. As a pastor, I empathize with Moses' burden. Over the years, I have encountered many individuals searching for God's will for their lives. They have sought advice on various matters, including job opportunities, parenting, career development, education, home buying, promotions, finding spouses, conflict resolution, relocation, intimacy, car purchasing, and many other life issues. Guiding God's people in discovering His will has always been essential to spiritual leadership.

Moses understood that understanding God's word was essential for discovering His will. "They come to me, and I decide between one person and another, and I make them know the statutes of God and His laws," Moses admitted. His father-in-law suggested that discerning God's will wasn't solely the responsibility of the leaders. He proposed gathering a group of informed, sincere believers to share this duty while reserving the most difficult issues for himself. Moses' experience demonstrates that discerning God's will can be challenging and complex.

Discovering God's will for our lives can feel like navigating a carnival maze of mirrors, where we continually bump into unseen walls while feeling our way toward what we hope is the exit. We all seek a map that guides us directly to the exit without wasting effort and emotion. Our search for God's will becomes even more complicated by confusion over what the exit looks like. What is God's will? Are we supposed to approach this search with a fatalistic outlook, assuming God is fully in control, and our task is to uncover the path He has already set as His will? We look for signs and confirmations, wondering how much freedom we have in expressing God's will. We attempt to distinguish between events that are destined to happen because of God's will and those that require our participation to come to pass. Or is everything predestined by God's will? We pray for His will, but often we remain uncertain about what an answer looks like. The more we want to please the Lord, the more we seek His will. Moses's role in guiding the people to discover God's will was complex and challenging. Paul believed that the first step in finding God's will requires total commitment.

If you're like most of us, finding God's will is closely connected to the significance of our decisions. We rarely pray about God's will when deciding what to buy while shopping. However, when thinking about a job change that takes us across the world, we pray and seek wise advice. In those cases, God's will becomes very important. We understand that pleasing Him means doing what He desires. The bigger the decision, the more we look for God's guidance. Paul's advice to the Romans highlights discovering God's will. To do this, we must commit, stand firm, and renew.

Seven years into my marriage, I began to question God's will. Nothing in my life had turned out the way I expected. Looking back, I see I was guilty of assuming that finding God's will meant getting what I wanted. I believed that if God loved me, He would grant the desires of my heart. I even cited Bible verses to support this belief: "Delight yourself in the Lord, and He will give you the desires of your heart" (Psalms 37:4). I thought that if God loved me, He would help me get into medical school, make me wealthy, improve my marriage, and lead me to success. Didn't the Bible teach this? The problem was that I had overlooked the first step in enjoying a relationship with Him. Later, as I grew closer to Him, I discovered that my wants and desires changed. As I studied the Bible, I came to understand that only part of God's will is fixed, while much of it depends on my obedience.

Reflect & Respond

As you finish this chapter, take a few quiet moments to reflect on what God might be speaking to your heart. These questions help you remember key truths, deepen your understanding, challenge your assumptions, and motivate you to action. Whether you're working through them alone or with a group, invite the Holy Spirit to guide your thoughts, encourage honest conversations, and reveal the next step in your walk with Christ. Let this be not just a review but a response of faith, obedience, and transformation.

1. What is the essential requirement for beginning a life that pleases God, and how does Paul illustrate the transformation when a person is born again?

2. Why is the gospel essential for understanding and living according to God's will, and what does it reveal about His desires for His people?

3. What role does the Holy Spirit play in guiding believers to understand and fulfill God's will, and how does this differ from simply following religious rules or formulas?

4. Why might sincere believers still struggle to discern God's will in specific situations, and how should they respond when clarity seems elusive?

5. How can increasing your understanding of God's will influence your everyday choices, relationships, and overall sense of purpose?

CHAPTER FOUR

FINDING GOD'S WILL

You were made for a purpose.
Until you find it, your life will always feel incomplete.
Rick Warren

One of my challenges has been confusing God's sovereign will with His desires. God's sovereign will is non-negotiable. Paul reminded the saints in Ephesus that God works out our salvation according to His plan. The Greek term used is *Boulen*, which reflects God's sovereign will. I don't understand every aspect of His sovereign will. The more I read about His will and compare it to the suffering in the world, the less I grasp its full meaning. Still, I know that the parts of God's sovereign will for my life will happen regardless of the circumstances.

> *In him we were also chosen, having been predestined according to the plan of him who works out everything in conformity with the purpose (Boulen) of his will (Thelema), in order that we, who were the first to hope in Christ, might be for the praise of his glory. (Ephesians 1:11-12)*
>
> *He chose (Boulen) to give us birth through the word of truth, that we might be a kind of firstfruits of all he created. (James 1:18)*

There is, however, another aspect of His will that significantly involves us. Traditionally, it has been called His "desirous will." This aspect of His will is expressed through the Greek word Thelema. It depends on our participation. God wants our marriages to reflect the love and respect of the Godhead; this happens only when we actively love our partners. God desires that each of our churches reach its full potential, but if only a few members get involved in serving, they will fall short of God's intended will. This aspect of God's will appears often in Scripture. God is not silent about His will for us; we can find it if we cooperate. He does not accomplish it in us without our cooperation. Understanding this helps us understand what Paul is explaining to the Romans. There are specific requirements for discovering God's will in our lives.

Until I understood what Scripture teaches about God's will, I didn't realize that my behavior and actions shape how His will is expressed in my life. When I studied Scripture, I learned that very little of God's will is about getting me into medical school or improving my marriage. Most of His will focuses on making me like His Son. It occurred to me that, regardless of where I was in life, being like Jesus was the most essential part of His will. This pleased the Lord. When I pleased Him, He fulfilled the desires of my heart that aligned with His wishes rather than my own. My marriage was struggling because I had stopped becoming more like God's Son. LouAnna was not the issue; I was. God hadn't called me to make LouAnna a better wife; He called me to become a better person and husband. God is determined to use every means to shape a likeness of His Son in me. He has the same goal for you if you have embraced the Gospel. That is what Paul was teaching when he wrote,

> And we know that in all things God works for the good of those who love him, who have been called according to his purpose. For those God foreknew he also predestined to be conformed to the likeness of his Son, that he might be the firstborn among many brothers. (Romans 8:28-29)

> And we, who with unveiled faces all reflect the Lord's glory, are being transformed into his likeness with ever-increasing glory, which comes from the Lord, who is the Spirit. (2 Corinthians 3:18)

Men and women who make a difference in their world as Christians are those who have discovered God's will for their lives. They actively pursue becoming more like Christ. In seeking this likeness, they have learned the "how."

Asking the right questions.

Years ago, I discussed the Lordship issues that sometimes divided the church with a friend. One group cited passages teaching that true believers cannot continue practicing sin while claiming to be followers of Jesus. The other camp believed that some believers are "carnal." They are saved but do not live in a way that reflects it. It was as if they accepted Jesus as their Savior but never made Him Lord of their lives.

"What are your thoughts on the Lordship issue?" I asked.

"It's an American thing," he said casually.

"No, it's a theological issue that divides the church." I started to wonder if he understood the problem.

He explained how he came to know the Lord as a young man. Raised in India, he ran home to tell his dad when he accepted Jesus as his savior. He found his dad reading the local newspaper in the living room. When he shared what had happened to him, his dad excused himself and left the room. A minute later, he re-entered with a loaded revolver.

Facing his son, he said, "You have five minutes to pack your things and leave. If you are here after that time, I will kill you."

My friend did not see his parents for the next fifteen years.

"Accepting Jesus in many parts of the world costs you something—sometimes, it costs you everything. Only in America is it socially acceptable to claim to be a believer while living as if you aren't. The Lordship issue is fundamentally an American issue," my friend explained. "Americans are independent and self-made. It costs them nothing to become a Christian. When they become believers, many resist being controlled by God's will," he said.

Being governed by His will was not always my desire. I

faced a conflict between wanting to follow my own path and accepting what God considers good for me. This raises one of life's fundamental questions: Who will decide what's good for you? You or God? Another person or God?

The primary thrust of the Devil's temptation is to suggest that we have the right to choose. In the Garden of Eden, Eve faced a similar challenge. Satan approached Eve and claimed that God knew that when she ate the fruit from the Tree of Knowledge of Good and Evil, she would become like God, able to decide what was good for herself. His deception centered on the idea that until that moment, God controlled what was good for Eve. If she ate the fruit, her eyes would be opened, and she could decide for herself what was good. After eating the fruit, Eve gave it to Adam. When Adam ate it, sin entered humanity, and humans began to struggle with who decides what is right. Usually, when Satan is involved, the temptation pushes us to act without trusting God's control. Do we want what's good for us or what's truly good? When God works in us, the two become the same. After the garden experience, we are left to decide what is best. How do we make the right choice?

In his book Decision Making and the Will of God, Gary Friesen proposes that we can determine God's will by asking two basic questions.

1. Is it Moral?
2. Is it wise?

These two questions reflect the wisdom of Paul's prayer to fill the Colossae believers with the knowledge of God's will "through spiritual wisdom and understanding" (Colossians 1:9). Is it moral? God never leads contrary to His Word. A pastor friend recounts meeting a couple who sought his marriage advice. Both were Christians and had met at a Christian camp earlier that week. They believed that God had orchestrated their meeting and thought it was His will for them to get married. The conversation went well for the first few minutes until the pastor realized they were already married to other believers!

"If you're already married, how can you think that marrying

each other would be God's will for you?" he asked incredulously.

"From the very first moment we met, we felt it was God's plan for us to be together." He explained that their desires did not come from God, as God's will is always moral and wise.

Wisdom is a challenging measurement. It is easier to tell what is not wise than what is.

Jeff was a young married man with a new family. He had a great job, a home, and a loving wife. He cherished both his church and his work. During the summer of his fifth year of marriage, he started to worry about living in the San Francisco Bay Area. His concerns weren't financial; instead, they came from a turmoil caused by an embellished dream.

Pastor, Linda and I are thinking about moving to Oregon. We hope you can help us understand God's will.

"Oh... do you have a job offer?" I asked, feeling a bit confused.

"No."

"Does Linda want to move?"

"Not exactly, but she will follow me wherever I go."

"What led to this decision?"

"I've always wanted to live in the Northwest."

"Have you ever been up there?"

"No, but we know some people who have relocated there, and they love it!"

I explained that God's will is always moral and wise. Although this wasn't an ethical issue, it seemed to lack wisdom. They planned to move to an unfamiliar place, leave a lucrative job, relocate with a wife who opposed the move, and separate from their families on both sides, all in hopes of finding employment, among other things. Before making this decision, I suggested they visit and assess the job market. I also recommended discussing this matter with family and friends to gather their opinions.

Fred ignored all advice and sought out advisors who would confirm his views. After moving to the Northwest, he spent months looking for work, only to return to California having lost his home, job, and dignity. God's will is wise.

When wisdom and morality come together in a decision, the outcome is acceptable to almost everyone. It reflects God's will. One of the first signs Fred should have noticed was a devout wife who found his decision unacceptable. Jeff's decision also revealed another flaw: it was somewhat immature. God's will is always "perfect" (Romans 12:2). This rich Greek word is most often translated as "mature." When we align ourselves with God's will, we find that maturity goes with us. God's will is consistently connected to what is mature. He never planned for us to stay in a state of immaturity or function with an adolescent mindset.

Experiencing God's will

How do you sense God's will in your life? Questions about whether a decision is moral and wise help us determine if it aligns with God's will. Still, the question remains: How do you sense God's will in your life? Once again, we turn to what Paul wrote to the Romans.

Therefore, I urge you, brothers, in view of God's mercy, to offer your bodies as living sacrifices, holy and pleasing to God--this is your spiritual act of worship. Do not conform any longer to the pattern of this world, but be transformed by the renewing of your mind. Then you will be able to test and approve what God's will is--his good, pleasing and perfect will. (Romans 12:1-2)

Finding God's will starts with offering our bodies as living sacrifices. Paul is not suggesting that we give our hearts to the Lord; he isn't asking for our lives, time, possessions, or anything except our bodies. When we give our bodies, we offer everything. When I give my body, I give Him my time, life, heart, and all that is connected to my existence in this body. On the surface, this command appears straightforward. However, obeying it becomes more complex as we begin to understand what it truly means to offer our bodies.

One benefit of living in America is the freedom to choose how we spend our time. In a recent conversation, I was reminded that time is the currency of our days. Finding time to care for our bodies is difficult for many of us. Before retiring from my pastoral role, I worked on recruiting hundreds of volunteers for essential ministry positions to help fulfill our church's mission. While speaking with numerous interested attendees, I discovered that many felt too overwhelmed to engage in ministry. From a pastor's perspective, many had added Christianity to their busy lives. They wanted to fit serving into their schedules, but couldn't remove anything already occupying their time. Offering their bodies was not feasible without making some sacrifices. Paul describes this offering as sacrificial, living, holy, pleasing, and worshipful.

The word "sacrificial" might seem intimidating; however, it embodies the core theme of Christianity. God sacrificed His Son, Jesus, to wipe away the record of our rebellion against Him. Jesus taught that "anyone who does not carry his cross and follow me cannot be my disciple" (Lk 14:27). Matthew elaborates on this idea as he quotes Jesus:

> . . . If anyone would come after me, he must deny himself and take up his cross and follow me. For whoever wants to save his life will lose it, but whoever loses his life for me will find it. What good will it be for a man if he gains the whole world, yet forfeits his soul? Or what can a man give in exchange for his soul? (Matthew 16:24-26)

Paul encouraged the saints at Colossae with the good news that believers should be joyfully thankful for being brought by God from darkness into His kingdom of light. This was achieved at a great sacrifice. It is reasonable for Paul and Jesus (and should be for every believer) to think that God expects His children to offer their bodies to Him as sacrifices. This comes at a cost. Herein lies the problem: offering our bodies does not simply mean adding another task to our busy schedules. Most of us continue to attempt to pile more onto an overloaded schedule. It fundamentally comes down to answering the question, "Who owns me?"

Every believer needs to know the answer. David understood this when he wrote, "The Lord is my shepherd." Joshua lived it through his challenge: "Who will you serve today? As for me and my family, we will serve the Lord." Peter encourages every believer to declare Jesus as Lord: "But in your hearts set apart Christ as Lord." (1 Pet 3:15). For Paul, offering our bodies as sacrifices to God makes perfect sense; it is our reasonable way of serving. As he writes to the Romans, he likely recalls the truth he shared with the Corinthians.

> *Do you not know that your body is a temple of the Holy Spirit, who is in you, whom you have received from God? You are not your own; you were bought at a price. Therefore honor God with your body. (1 Corinthians 6:19-20)*

The word Paul uses, "bought," is often translated as "redeemed." He employs the term *agorazo,* which means to pay a ransom by purchasing slaves from the market. (*Trenches synonyms*) The focus of this word is on being purchased. Slavery was a common reality throughout the Roman Empire, as Paul notes. Slaves were bought and sold in markets. Paul uses this powerful language to remind us that, at one time, we all were slaves to sin. When we were in sin, God showed His great love for us through the sacrifice of His Son on our behalf (Romans 5:8). When the early church read *agorazo,* they understood the implication of someone paying the price for them. In his letter to the Galatians, Paul reminded believers that, in God's timing, He redeemed them from under the law (Galatians 4:4). Here, instead of using *agorazo,* he uses *exagorazo.* Not only had they been purchased, but their purchase also freed them from the slave market. Paul and Peter introduce us to a third word translated as "redeem," *apolutrou.*

> *Who gave himself for us to redeem [apolutrou] us from all wickedness and to purify for himself a people that are his very own, eager to do what is good. (Titus 2:14)*

> *For you know that it was not with perishable things such as silver*

or gold that you were redeemed [apolutrou] from the empty way of life handed down to you from your forefathers,   but with the precious blood of Christ, a lamb without blemish or defect. (1Pet. 1:18-19)

The focus of this term is that we were not only bought out of bondage and removed from the slave market, but we were also set free and granted liberty. This redemptive language is essential for understanding Paul's call in Romans 12:1-2.

Before beginning chapter 12, Paul spent eleven chapters explaining that people are naturally sinful and separated from God. However, as Paul writes, God demonstrated His love for us by allowing Christ to die for us while we were still sinful. Accepting this truth brings us into God's family. When we are born again, we receive the Holy Spirit, who becomes our guide, source of strength, and prayer partner in the Christian journey. It is reasonable for us to worship Him by offering our bodies as holy and pleasing sacrifices.

God could have forced us to do this, but He gave us the freedom to dedicate our bodies. Paul uses the Greek word "paristemi" to describe our commitment. Paristemi is defined as "to make something available" (Greek-English Lexicon of the New Testament). The first step in finding God's will is to obey this command. However, too often, we believe that accepting Jesus as our Savior is all that's required. We become like Helen, a fictional character that Marty Trammell and I used in our book, Spiritual Fitness.

Helen was so busy running her business that she lacked time to focus on her spiritual life. She was deeply involved in marketing and making money. She pretended she didn't need to face spiritual issues, using her busy schedule as an excuse to avoid change. Lost in her daily tasks, she didn't realize her business was already leading her toward divorce. Her son grew up with a nanny, a part-time dad, and an absent mother. Although she sensed something was wrong, her focus remained on making her mark in the business world. She believed she would find time to fix things once the company went public. But the business required her presence during the transition to the stock market. After it was over, she pushed her problems to the back of her mind. The emptiness in her neglected marriage and the home she left behind pushed her to devote even more time to her business. The sad cycle continued—until one day, Helen had lunch with her son, Brook.

Brook sat across from Helen at the Ritz-Carlton. Brook had just graduated from college, and Helen reflected on how quickly time had passed. He began telling his mom about his "conversion" to Christianity. While expressing his profound need for a Savior, his mom dropped a bombshell: she had made the same decision in college!

"What?" Brook pushed his coffee cup to the middle of the table.

"During my junior year, I joined a Campus Life group and accepted Christ as my Savior."

"How did I never know this?"

"By the time you reached high school, your father and I had separated, and I was adding a new warehouse..." She gently wiped her lipstick with the linen napkin.

"Mom, are you sure you're saved?"

Hours later, on her flight home, Helen couldn't shake the question: "Was she a Christian?" If her family never knew, maybe she wasn't. If Helen was a Christian, only God and she knew... and she had her doubts.

As the days passed, Helen slowly lost interest in "the business." The question kept coming up. While reviewing each day's accounts, she realized that her spiritual records didn't match. No matter how hard she tried, she couldn't reconcile the books.

After another restless night of sleep, Helen reached out to one of her former executives. She remembered an incident from years ago when Anderson declined a major promotion because of his role as an elder in his church. At the time, she thought, "How foolish."

Anderson was surprised by the telephone call. He remembered her clearly and agreed she could come over despite being late. No, she wasn't disturbing him. Anderson and his wife, Lisa, prayed for Helen in their living room. They had no idea why she was coming, but she was. Anderson didn't even know if Helen remembered that he had lost his job with her company for refusing that promotion. All he knew was that he could hear the panic in her voice, which he assumed was related to the new merger.

Anderson saw a desperate woman standing on his porch when he answered the doorbell. It was obvious she hadn't slept in quite some time. Helen was known for being in charge and composed, so what could have caused her to break down like this? Anderson wondered.

Over the next hour, Helen reflected on the past few weeks. "Mom, are you sure you're saved?" The question haunted her. Anderson was the only employee she could recall who could answer it.

That moment changed Helen's life. For the first time in her successful career, she realized her business was a distraction that kept her from becoming the person God intended her to be. For the first time, she understood Anderson's decision to turn down the promotion. As Anderson guided her in Christ's offer of salvation, a new life flowed through her veins and into her books.

Helen chose to offer her body as a sacrifice to God. Anderson explained that this was the logical choice for a believer worshiping Him. In many ways, we resemble Helen: hidden believers who never fully commit to God's plan for our lives but still seek to uncover His will. We desire His blessings, even though our lives do not please Him. We assume He speaks figuratively when Jesus invites us to take His yoke and carry a cross. However, Anderson told Helen that Jesus was being literal. His message was clear: You cannot serve me without commitment. Paul reminds us that the first step to being filled with the will of God is total commitment, including our time, resources, and priorities.

I think of my dad when I reflect on role models and time management. Early in my marriage, my dad was preparing for retirement. He and my mom had bought a piece of property in a Sierra Mountains community in Northern California. The drive from the Bay Area to their property took over three hours. Every Friday after work, my mom and dad would pack the car and head to their property. They would arrive around 9:00 PM and work for a few hours before staying at a local motel. On Saturday, they spent the whole day building their retirement home. They would leave the property around 8:00 PM and head back home. One day after church, I asked my dad why he didn't just stay on Sunday, suggesting it would help him finish the home faster.

He said, "I have to be in church on Sundays."

"God understands if you miss a few Sundays to complete your home," I said.

"I'm not trying to impress God. I committed to teaching a boys' Sunday School class and want to stay faithful. I also serve as a leader in the church, and it's impossible to lead from afar. Being dedicated to the Body of Christ matters to me. My neighbors observe our lives, and I want to send the right message."

My dad realized that offering his body as worship required dedicating his time. Stephen Covey helps us better understand our relationship with time. How do we allocate our time? Covey suggests that a successful person views time in terms of importance and urgency rather than just focusing on tasks. (Stephen R. Covey. The 7 Habits of Highly Effective People, Powerful Lessons in Personal Change. page 151) Many of us are driven by what is urgent.

His model shows that urgent matters fall into two categories: important and unimportant. We spend most of our time in area I (urgent and important), III (urgent but unimportant), and IV (neither important nor urgent). While some time should be devoted to quadrants I and III, very little should be allocated to IV. A wise person learns to invest more time in quadrant II, where things are important but not urgent, at least not yet. The most critical area of our time management is often overlooked because it involves important issues that are not urgent. Since they are not urgent, we tend to postpone them. Only when they become urgent do we devote our time and interest; however, it is often too late.

We need to move our commitment into quadrant one. Paul stresses that offering ourselves to the Lord is urgent and essential. Without taking this first step, we can't grasp God's will. But, time isn't the only thing we should focus on; offering ourselves also involves dedicating all our resources to Him.

Reflect & Respond

As you finish this chapter, take a few quiet moments to reflect on what God might be speaking to your heart. These questions help you remember key truths, deepen your understanding, challenge your assumptions, and motivate you to action. Whether you're working through them alone or with a group, invite the Holy Spirit to guide your thoughts, encourage honest conversations, and reveal the next step in your walk with Christ. Let this be not just a review but a response of faith, obedience, and transformation.

1. What are the two aspects of God's will discussed in the chapter, and how do the Greek words Boulen and Thelema help clarify their meanings?

2. According to Romans 12:1-2, what is the first step to experiencing God's will, and how does Paul describe offering our bodies as "living sacrifices"?

3. Why is giving ourselves to God described as sacrificial instead of just a simple addition to our lives, and how does this relate to understanding God's redemptive work through Christ?

4. What fundamental question lies at the heart of the struggle with God's will, and how do Gary Friesen's two questions clarify the pursuit of God's guidance?

5. How does aligning with God's will contribute to spiritual maturity, and in what ways is maturity a key indicator of a life increasingly shaped by God's desires rather than by cultural expectations?

CHAPTER FIVE

KEEPING THE MAIN THING
THE MAIN THING

Your life changes when your priorities
shift to what truly matters –
God, love, and purpose.
(Anonymous)

The first step in dedicating our bodies to the Lord is prioritizing our lives. It took me years to truly understand how my dad lived. Looking back, I realize he had figured out how to "put first things first" (Covey). I was in first grade and living in Oakland, California. I remember that day well. When school ended, I walked home and saw my mom and dad sitting on the living room couch as I opened the front door. I had never seen my dad home from work during the day, so I sensed something was wrong. They told me we were moving to Bend, Oregon, to help my grandparents. My grandparents owned a chicken ranch and a business, but were struggling and facing bankruptcy. Mom and Dad sold our house, used our savings, and moved to support my mom's parents.

Over the next few years, my parents bought the business from my grandparents, paid off all their debts, revitalized it, created a future business plan, and built a new home for themselves. Suddenly, one morning, my grandmother told my parents that they were no longer welcome. To move back home, my parents had to borrow money for the trip and start fresh in Northern California. I felt very angry with my grandparents for how they treated my mom and dad. While driving back to California in the moving van, my dad sensed my anger and encouraged me to share my feelings. He shared his perspective when I reminded him of how unfairly we were treated.

"Son, your grandparents are the only parents your mom has. They called us because they needed help. We met that need, and now it's time for the next chapter in our lives."

"But we lost all our money and have nothing—what was it all for?" I said.

My Dad responded, "None of what we had was truly ours. God used us to help Grandma and Grandpa. He will provide for our needs. We did what was right."

That experience is deeply engraved in my memory. My dad understood that surrendering our bodies to the Lord required everything we had. I also observed a set of priorities in my dad that influenced his decision-making. These are equally essential if we are to fully commit to the Lord.

Paul reasonably asks us to commit. God is not a bully. He could have saved us and required us to offer our bodies as living, holy, and pleasing sacrifices. But as His children, He desires us to commit ourselves willingly. He asks us to change our priorities so our lives reflect the transformation from being slaves to being His free children. Still, like Eric and Cynthia, many of us take too long to make that commitment.

Eric and Cynthia have been members of the Hillsdale Community Fellowship for several years. They have been Christians since childhood, raised in stable Christian homes, and have enjoyed successful careers. Like their parents, they are intensely focused on their pursuits, leaving them little time for anything else. Eric scheduled a meeting with his pastor to discuss his growing concerns.

While sitting in his pastor's office, Eric admitted to being consumed by the desire to build a successful business and secure a stable financial future. Deep inside him, a growing doubt gnawed at whether he was on the right path. The sermons from the past few weeks have concentrated on making the most of life, carrying one's cross, and setting aside self.

After hearing Eric's concerns, the pastor shared a well-known story with him.

A philosophy professor stood before his class with several items arranged in front of him. As the class began in silence, he picked up a large, empty mayonnaise jar and filled it with rocks about 2 inches in diameter. He then asked the students if the jar was full, and they agreed that it was.

The professor then picked up a box of pebbles and poured them into the jar, shaking it gently. Naturally, the pebbles settled into the gaps between the rocks. He then asked the students again whether the jar was full. They agreed that it was.

The students laughed as the professor picked up a box of sand and poured it into the jar. Of course, the sand filled everything else. "Now,' said the professor, 'I want you to understand that this represents your life. The rocks signify the important things—your family, partner, health, and children—anything so vital to you that losing it would nearly destroy you. The pebbles represent other significant matters, like your job, house, and car. The sand constitutes everything else: the little stuff.

'If you put the sand in the jar first, there isn't any room for the pebbles or the rocks. The same applies to your life. If you allocate all your energy and time to the small stuff, you'll never make space for the things that truly matter to you. Focus on what's essential for your happiness. Spend time playing with your children. Make time for medical checkups. Take your partner out dancing. There will always be time for work, cleaning the house, hosting dinner parties, and fixing the disposal. Prioritize the rocks first – the significant things.'

As the pastor asked questions about priorities and putting first things first, Eric began to realize that he had overlooked the "big rocks" in his life. He left the meeting convinced that he had been chasing his dream rather than God's. He now understood the importance of significantly realigning his priorities.

Eric's condition reflects our culture and many aspects of our lives. We rush through life, uncertain about what truly matters. At the end of our lives, we realize our jars are missing many essential rocks. For Christians, the Bible guides us regarding our priorities. We can easily overlook Paul's call to offer our bodies as living sacrifices. However, we cannot fully experience God's will without this boulder in our jar.

Establishing biblical priorities is the first step in ensuring we have the right boulders in our jar. The ability of believers to live according to God's will is demonstrated by their capacity to develop biblical priorities as they dedicate their bodies to Him. Paul told the Ephesians, "Be very careful, then, how you live—not as unwise but as wise, making the most of every opportunity, because the days are evil." (Ephesians 5:15-16)

Paul warns us to be cautious and vigilant in our daily lives. He urges us to walk thoughtfully as we seize every opportunity. He encourages us to see each chance as a transaction that must be handled wisely. Time is money. We need to approach this with purpose because the days are filled with difficulties.

What you will become is already beginning to take shape. What are your priorities? Setting them based on biblical principles is the first step toward dedicating your body. Maybe you feel like your jar is filled with sand and pebbles, and now you see the rocks around you that don't fit. It's time to empty your jar and start placing the rocks inside. It's never too late.

Life's priorities shape our behavior. Changes within the inner self influence our entire being and affect our actions. When the heart changes, the person changes. The Bible teaches Christians to prioritize their lives by dedicating their bodies. This is a rational act of spiritual worship. The priorities from such dedication form the fabric of authentic Christianity. When you meet genuine believers, you don't see individual threads; you see the whole fabric of authenticity. All these threads must be present; they are closely linked. If one is missing, authenticity is lost.

Priority: Spiritual over material

Our priorities distinguish us from the unsaved world. If our concerns are the same as those of the world, we need to reassess what truly matters. If our solutions to problems match those of our non-Christian neighbors, then our priorities are out of sync.

Christ emphasized this priority while teaching his disciples.

> So do not worry, saying, "What shall we eat?" or "What shall we drink?" or "What shall we wear?" For the pagans run after all these things, and your heavenly Father knows that you need them. But seek first his kingdom and his righteousness, and all these things will be given to you as well. (Matthew 6:31-33)

We live in a society that values hard work and the pursuit of wealth. In his book, "Man in the Mirror," Patrick Morley concludes that many American Christian men are cultural Christians rather than genuine biblical believers. They have embraced the American Dream, overlooking the fact that spiritual matters should take priority over material concerns.

Several years ago, I met a young man who resigned from a prominent position at a major corporation to spend more time with his family. His decision came while he was sitting on a plane over the Atlantic, having just finished a trip during which he spent 43 hours on several flights. While reading his Bible, he asked himself, "In what way am I fulfilling God's mandate for my life?" He concluded that he had misspent his time and realized the spiritual priority of the spiritual over the material.

Where we invest our time and money shows how much we value this priority. It is surprising how little time many of us actually spend demonstrating our spiritual commitment. Church attendance is just the basic way we express this priority. At a pastor's conference, George Barna noted that when "committed Christians" were asked how often they attended church, most said they went regularly. But when asked how many weeks per month they usually attended, they said less than 3 out of 4! If true, the average "committed" Christian misses more than 3 months of church each year.

These statistics surprise me. I once belonged to a service club while living in Salem, Oregon. Each time I missed a meeting, I was fined! What we often overlook is that every time we fail to gather as Christians, we suffer a loss. This loss shows up as reduced impact and benefits from involvement. The writer of Hebrews warns, "Let us not give up meeting together, as some are in the habit of doing, but let us encourage one another – and all the more as you see the Day approaching." (Hebrews 10:25) Pleasing the Lord involves using our gifts to equip and minister to other believers. Being present fosters a maturity that cannot develop in our absence (Ephesians 4:11-16). Our commitment to this spiritual priority is also demonstrated through our giving.

I served as a pastor in a church where our giving was above average. When we compared our contributions with those of other churches of similar size, we often ranked at the top. However, this comparison was flawed. The proper benchmark measures our giving against our capacity to give. When evaluated by this standard, most of us are "Christian tippers." We reach into our pockets and give whatever loose change or bills we can find. This is rarely a sacrificial act. Studies show that the average church member contributes less than 3% of their income to the church. In my experience, 20% of the members give 80% of the church's offerings, 50% contribute 20%, and 30% give nothing. Although our church's giving was above average, it still fell short of our actual capacity to give. If we had prioritized our giving based on this understanding, our contributions could have increased significantly. We cannot expect God's approval when our giving shows a lack of personal commitment to Him. Still, we continue to anticipate His blessings.

Jesus reminds us that where our treasure is, "there your heart will be also." (Matthew 6:21) He concludes, "No one can serve two masters. Either he will hate the one and love the other, or he will be devoted to the one and despise the other. You cannot serve God and Money." (Matthew 6:24)

One of the top priorities is "spiritual over material." Setting this priority is the first step in dedicating our bodies to the Lord. Making this commitment requires purpose; it means actively taking initiative rather than remaining passive.

Priority: Active over Passive.

Years ago, a close friend died from a brain tumor. She had arranged her funeral, selecting the music, the speaker, and all the attendees. Although she didn't want to die, she was prepared. She and her husband were active members of their church and community, making a significant difference in LouAnna's and my lives, as well as in the lives of those around them. Her husband and I served together on the church leadership team. Her funeral was attended by people whose lives had been touched by this couple. They came from diverse backgrounds, including neighbors and many fellow church members. This couple had a positive impact on everyone.

As I sat there reflecting on how much she would be missed, I realized their impact was intentional. They planned it. They approached things proactively, seizing every opportunity. They kept a balance, managing their time so that God's ministry and their family came first, while still supporting those around them who needed help. They were actively involved in all areas of life.

In the conclusion of his letter to Titus, Paul emphasizes the importance of prioritizing activity over passivity.

This is a trustworthy saying. And I want you to stress these things, so that those who have trusted in God may be careful to devote themselves to doing what is good. These things are excellent and profitable for everyone. (Titus 3:8)

Our role as believers is to be proactive in our Christianity. Paul encouraged the saints at Philippi to work out their "salvation with fear and trembling, for it is God who works in you to will and to act according to his good purpose." (Philippians 2:12-13) Paul does not imply that we can save ourselves through our own efforts. Theologians discuss the three tenses of salvation: we have been saved from the penalty of sin, we are being saved from the power of sin, and we will be saved in the future from the presence of sin. We are actively involved in the current stage of being saved from sin's power. This approach requires proactivity rather than passivity, allowing events to unfold. We actively maintain our spiritual well-being and nurture healthy attitudes that please the Lord.

Priority: Serving over Sitting

God has blessed us to serve. It feels strange to call our gathering "church services." How can I serve while I'm sitting in a seat that is being served? Attending is just the beginning. Being present and listening to the Word offers great benefits. But we are called to serve. We are encouraged to be "doers" of the Word. The Bible is full of encouraging words on this topic.

> In the same way, faith by itself, if it is not accompanied by action, is dead. (James 4:17)

> Each one should use whatever gift he has received to serve others, faithfully administering God's grace in its various forms. (1 Peter 4:10)

God's will is connected to our participation. God wants every church to succeed, but many will not. If half of those attending choose not to engage, participate actively, and use their gifts, then without His miraculous help, the church will fall short of what God desires. We are in a divine partnership, and God expects us to work. He wants us to shift from being passive to active in our faith and service. He will energize us, but we must act. This idea guided Paul's ministry.

> We proclaim him, admonishing and teaching everyone with all wisdom, so that we may present everyone perfect in Christ. To this end I labor, struggling with all his energy, which so powerfully works in me. (Colossians 1:28-29)

This thought should guide our ministry. We can't make a

difference without taking action. A sailor friend once took me sailing and said that the rudder can't steer the boat unless it moves. If we do nothing, we become like an idle boat, drifting aimlessly without a clear direction. Simply being good isn't enough. You can be good your whole life and still never make a difference. To make an impact, we must engage and focus on action. Doing so will help us clarify our next steps.

Priority: Model over mouth

Have you ever wondered why the unchurched world holds such a poor opinion of Christianity? A pastor friend shared a story about asking two questions to several people who were antagonistic toward Christianity. The first question was, "What are your thoughts when you hear the name 'Jesus'?" Everyone in the room had something positive to say. The second question was, "What are your thoughts when you hear the word 'Christian'?" This time, everyone in the room had something negative to say. Why the disconnect? Why do those who represent Jesus have such a different reputation? In his book, *Soul Salsa*, Leonard Sweet makes a remarkable statement.

> If George Barna's research is to be believed, over half of all unchurched people say they want to find a closer, personal relationship with God. They don't know how to find it. Barna's conclusion: 'These are not people who are anti-religion. These are people who, for the most part, believe in some kind of god or deity. They haven't been able to figure out, How I make it real . . . in my life' (pages 10-11)

One apparent reason why unchurched people struggle to connect with God's love is that they have seen very few examples. This is why some who oppose Christianity can praise Jesus while criticizing Christians.

A man once accused me of firing him because he was a Christian. While managing the hospital lab, I dismissed him. His understanding of Christianity influenced his termination. John was open about his faith and made a public issue of working on Sundays. One of the rules our technicians agreed to when joining the hospital was their commitment to share weekend shifts. Hospitals operate 24/7, so someone must be there to care for patients. Out of more than 30 technicians, John was the only one who refused to work his share of Sundays. Several other technologists were also Christians, but they chose not to turn working every third Sunday into a controversy. Not John. His refusal to work Sundays was both public and principled.

To make matters worse, John was a terrible employee. He was married but interacted with women at the hospital as if he were single. He didn't wear a wedding ring because he claimed it caused a rash. He had several affairs with employees from other departments, which became common knowledge. I spoke to him privately several times about the gap between his words and actions. He would publicly share his faith while living as if he had none. This behavior made all of us angry and harmed our testimonies. I have acted similarly before and was even more sensitive to his blatant hypocrisy.

One afternoon, my hematology supervisor approached me with a concern about John's performance. She observed that it took him significantly longer than the other techs to draw inpatient blood work, so she kept a log. When I asked if she had spoken to him about the issue, she said she had.

"Well, what did he say?" I asked. As the words left my mouth, I sensed she was hesitant to go there.

"What?" I exclaimed!

"You know he is a Christian..."

I thought, "Oh brother!"

"When he meets patients with spiritual needs, he feels he should... You know... whatever you Christians do when you corner people and try to convince them that they need Jesus... I'm sorry, I don't want to offend you," she stammered.

"And how many patients has he met that have spiritual needs?" I asked cynically.

"Well, all of them today."

Over the next several months, we discussed John's

performance. Complaints came from the medical staff, the nursing staff, and the patients, all raising concerns about John's assertiveness in sharing his faith. After several months without any change in his behavior, I decided to let him go. In our final meeting, he accused me of betraying the cause of Christ. I explained that a person's strongest testimony begins with being a credible role model. It always starts with authenticity, as people look there first. The simple truth was that John conveyed one message while embodying another.

The world is looking for someone who truly reflects Jesus's essence. The Holy Spirit plays a vital role in developing this in our lives. Genuine people are those who make a difference. They are dedicated workers who earn the right to share their faith. Their lives are open books. Their words and actions show that they follow Jesus.

Priority: Prayer before action

It has taken me years to break a bad habit, but I sometimes slip back into it. My problem is leaving God out of the picture until I'm desperate. When facing challenges, I tend to act instead of worry; I am a planner. My actions always start with a plan, which I refine until I reach a dead end; then I pray. One of the most important habits we can develop is to pray, act, and then pray again in that order. This pattern is seen throughout Scripture. In Nehemiah's life, the process of praying, acting, and praying is shown in the first two chapters bearing his name. In chapter one of Nehemiah, he prays after learning that the wall in Jerusalem remains unfinished. There are four months between chapter one and chapter two, during which he develops a strategy to fix the problem without revealing to the king that he's worried about the wall. After four months, he feels the time is right, and he shares his concern about Jerusalem with the king. The king asks for an explanation, and the text shows that Nehemiah prays again.

The king said to me, 'What is it you want?' Then I prayed to the

God of heaven, and I answered the king, . . . (Nehemiah 2:4)

When he heard the king's question, he did what most of us do in similar situations: silently said a quick prayer for help before answering the king. As a result of his prayer, the king funded the trip back to Jerusalem.

Prayer is a teaching of the Bible that is often neglected or misused. It is overlooked when we act without praying and misapplied when we pray for things God has already given us the strength to accomplish ourselves. I wrote this section while ministering to a local church in Vienna, Austria. I was about to drive with the pastor into town for my last session. It would have been a misuse of prayer for me to think that, instead of getting up, opening the door, walking upstairs, opening the front door, walking down to the car, and getting in, I should pray for God to miraculously transport me from the pastor's study to the vehicle. God rarely uses prayer to achieve what He has already equipped us to do. When we pray, it is a form of divine cooperation. Nehemiah understood this. He prayed, planned, acted, prayed again, and kept on acting. He did not just pray.

"Pastor, I haven't found a job and I need one badly," Jim said in frustration

The small company where Jim had worked for twenty years was closing down. He had lost his job and remained unemployed for several weeks. Like many of us, he was just one paycheck away from homelessness. During our conversation, I learned he had stopped actively searching for a new job and was instead spending hours praying about his situation. His marriage was now falling apart.

Marge, his wife, had never worked outside the home. When Jim announced that he had lost his job, she began searching for work. She found a position as a receptionist at a local real estate office. Although the job didn't replace Jake's previous salary, it ensured the mortgage was paid and food was on the table. She would come home from work each night and ask Jim, "What did you do today?" Jim realized she was asking, "Did you look for a job today?" He had searched during the first couple of weeks with no luck. Discouraged, he spent his days watching TV and sleeping. As we sat in my office, I said.

Jim, here's what you need to do. Starting tomorrow, after a brief prayer, you will begin your job search. You will leave the house at 8:00 am. Throughout the morning, distribute as many resumes as possible and complete as many applications as you can. Take a lunch break and continue the same process in the afternoon until around 5:00 pm. When you return home, you and Marge will review your efforts and pray that God will bless them. By making job hunting your focus, you allow God to bless your efforts.

Jim followed my advice. Over the next three weeks, several things happened. First, he experienced a peace he had never known before, deciding to make job hunting his full-time focus. He was doing everything he could and trusting God to bless his efforts. Second, he and Marge no longer argued about the issue. Marge realized that he was doing all he could. Finally, Jim secured a job.

In his Epistle, James reminds us that during difficult times, we can always pray for wisdom, and God will give it generously without hesitation (James 1:5). One of the most important behavioral priorities we can establish is staying active in prayer. Even though it is the hardest thing we do, it is also the most rewarding.

Priority: Growth over comfort.

"I wanted to meet with you, Pastor, because I am having trouble with a job change and want to understand God's will for me," Neal said over the phone.

Neal was an intelligent businessman with a bright future. He grew up in the San Francisco Bay Area and had lived there most of his 32 years, except for a few years he spent in college. Like many people, Neal was concerned with discovering God's will, which he believed lay ahead. Usually, we focus most on God's will when making significant decisions. Asking if our choices are moral and wise helps us understand God's will. Neal and I considered whether this new job was a wise decision.

"My education and experience have prepared me for this job; it has to be God's will."

"Neal, have you ever thought that maybe God's will in this situation is more about shaping your character than about the job itself? We don't know if God cares whether you get this job, but we do know that whether you do or not, God wants to develop the character of His Son in you. He wants you to resemble Jesus."

Later, Neal called to tell me he didn't get the job. He felt disappointed but saw it as a chance to grow. He said, "Growing is painful."

God uses the experiences in our lives to shape Christlikeness within us. (Romans 8:28-29) The strong desire of God, His will, is to make us like His Son. It may not relate to where we work, where we live, or whom we marry; it consistently involves who we resemble. I don't always enjoy the process, but the Bible has much to say about this journey.

> Not only so, but we also rejoice in our sufferings, because we know that suffering produces perseverance; perseverance, character, and character, hope. (Romans 5:4-5)

> These [trials] have come so that your faith... may be proved genuine... (1 Peter 1:7)

The issue with this process is that it seldom occurs within our comfort zone. God values our growth more than our comfort. He also prioritizes our character over any achievements.

In the book "I Want to Change, So Help Me God" by James MacDonald, the author distinguishes between growth and change. Growth is a long-term process that slowly moves us toward maturity, step by step. It presumes we are on the right path. Change, on the other hand, is an immediate call to action. It commands, "The boat is sinking, bail!" Many of us confuse growth and change.

Some issues we don't "grow out of." Some things in our lives need to change. Angry people rarely grow out of their anger; they must change before they can produce. I have met many men and women who reached old age without ever changing a character flaw that haunted them until the end. God is concerned with our growth, and the first step is to change us. Neither process happens in the comfort zone.

Christ met a man sitting by the fountain of Bethsaida who was an invalid and asked him, "Do you want to be healed?" (John 5). I once thought he was asking a rhetorical question. Who wouldn't want to be healed after being handicapped for 38 years? But I realized that it was a sincere question. For 38 years, he had depended on others to meet his needs. If Jesus healed him, he would have to take responsibility for his well-being. It was a sincere question.

Dr. Phillip McGraw asks his counselees, "Is it working?" Is it working for you? If not, step out of your comfort zone, make a change, and start to grow. God wants this to happen. When it does, you will demonstrate the character that God is seeking.

Priority: Character over accomplishment

Several years ago, I learned about a church that appointed a man as their Senior Pastor despite his history of multiple affairs. The fact that he had been asked to resign from his previous ministry due to an affair with a secretary did not alter the pulpit committee's decision when selecting him for this new church. They chose him because he had successfully led small congregations to grow into larger ones. He was excellent at delivering sermons. The church grew to over a thousand members within the first two years. During his fifth year, he had another affair and was once again asked to leave. When he left, he took several hundred followers with him to start a new church. They continued to believe in him because his preaching abilities blinded them. He had remarkable skills but lacked character.

The Bible teaches that character is the foundation and key to receiving God's blessing. According to the Bible, churches grow because God "adds to their number." A Christ-like man or woman demonstrates strong character. In God's plan, character takes precedence over achievement.

I remain skeptical of the church growth formula that ignores the character principle. I also doubt parenting models that focus on achievement without acknowledging the importance of character and role modeling. To succeed, we must prioritize character over achievement. In God's eyes, a man or woman with character and abilities will leave a more lasting impact than someone with great skills but little character.

Our priorities are significant. People who dedicate themselves to the Lord begin by establishing biblical priorities. In our effort to please God, offering our bodies as living sacrifices is just the first step toward discovering God's will for our lives. The subsequent steps involve challenging cultural beliefs and renewing our minds with God's teachings about life.

Reflect & Respond

As you finish this chapter, take a few quiet moments to reflect on what God might be speaking to your heart. These questions help you remember key truths, deepen your understanding, challenge your assumptions, and motivate you to action. Whether you're working through them alone or with a group, invite the Holy Spirit to guide your thoughts, encourage honest conversations, and reveal the next step in your walk with Christ. Let this be not just a review but a response of faith, obedience, and transformation.

1. Why does Paul encourage Christians to present their bodies as living, holy, and pleasing sacrifices to God? How does this demonstrate a believer's commitment to spiritual priorities over material ones?

2. What do the professor's jar illustration (rocks, pebbles, sand) and the story of Eric and Cynthia reveal about how Christians often misplace their priorities? What adjustments are needed to align with God's will?

3. How does Paul describe the Christian way of life in Ephesians 5:15-16, and what do the statistics on church attendance and giving reveal about the commitment level among many believers today?

4. What does it mean to "work out your salvation with fear and trembling" (Philippians 2:12-13), and how can this mindset affect your daily choices, spiritual growth, and responsiveness to God's will?

5. Why does the author emphasize growth over comfort and character over accomplishment in the Christian life, particularly in leadership, and what biblical principles support this view?

CHAPTER SIX

RESIST AND RENEW

We must learn to live in the world but not be shaped by it,
to think with Scripture rather than absorb
the assumptions of the age.
John Stott

Do not conform any longer to the pattern of this world,
but be transformed by the renewing of your mind. Then
you will be able to test and approve what God's will is—
his good, pleasing and perfect will.
(Romans 12:2)

Paul warns against conforming to the world's mold, choosing the Greek word *aión* over the more common term *kosmos*. Scripture teaches that *kosmos* is ruled by Satan and is designed to thwart God's redemptive plan for creation. We are cautioned not to love it because doing so diminishes our love for the Father. James warns that friendship with the world is a significant source of conflict in a believer's life. Paul uses the term *aión* to remind us to resist adopting the world's motivations and methods. *Aión* refers to a span of time or an age. Paul's use of this term in his introduction to the letter to the Galatian church helps us understand why we should resist conforming to the mold of this age, as Christ rescued us from the present evil age, *aion* (Galatians 1:4). Being influenced by the culture in which we live has always posed a challenge for God's people.

As Israel left Egypt and traveled toward the Promised Land,

they were reminded not to adopt the customs of the nations they encountered. When they finally took possession of the land promised by God, they were once again warned to avoid being influenced by the peoples around them. Seeing that other nations had kings, they sought one for themselves. Although God intended to appoint a king over Israel, the people wanted to be like the surrounding nations; so, He relented and gave them Saul. This tendency to imitate those around us continued to affect the early church. Once again, God issued several warnings to His children.

You adulterous people, don't you know that friendship with the world is hatred toward God? Anyone who chooses to be a friend of the world becomes an enemy of God. (James 4:4)

So I tell you this, and insist on it in the Lord, that you must no longer live as the Gentiles do, in the futility of their thinking. They are darkened in their understanding and separated from the life of God because of the ignorance that is in them due to the hardening of their hearts. Having lost all sensitivity, they have given themselves over to sensuality so as to indulge in every kind of impurity, with a continual lust for more. (Ephesians 4:17-19)

Do not love the world or anything in the world. If anyone loves the world, the love of the Father is not in him. For everything in the world—the cravings of sinful man, the lust of his eyes and the boasting of what he has and does—comes not from the Father but from the world. The world and its desires pass away, but the man who does the will of God lives forever. (1 John 2:15-17)

One of the biggest cultural appeals for believers is American culture. Our guaranteed freedoms stand out, and it's easy to be influenced by our way of life. The biblical roots of our nation, along with a capitalistic economic mindset, can seem like a good match for Christianity. However, our culture often views Christianity merely as a religion, which it is not. Christianity has always been about a relationship, and this concept underpins Peter's reminder of who we are.

But you are a chosen people, a royal priesthood, a holy nation, a people belonging to God, that you may declare the praises of him who called you out of darkness into his wonderful light. Once you were not a people, but now you are the people of God; once you had not received mercy, but now you have received mercy. Dear friends, I urge you, as aliens and strangers in the world, to abstain from sinful desires, which war against your soul. Live such good lives among the pagans that, though they accuse you of doing wrong, they may see your good deeds and glorify God on the day he visits us. (1 Peter 2:9-12)

Peter's confession is powerful. We are chosen, royal, and priests, creating God's nation within our own. We have been pulled from darkness into His light; our purpose is to represent Him. We demonstrate this by being different and not conforming to the American way. We are "aliens and strangers in the world."

As aliens and strangers, we represent a different country and culture. We stand for God. We do this by living such good lives that even if they criticize us, those around us see our positive impact and glorify God. This passage may seem like an overstatement when considered alone, but it is not. It reflects teachings found throughout the scriptures. This is what Jesus taught in the Sermon on the Mount.

You are the salt of the earth. But if the salt loses its saltiness, how can it be made salty again? It is no longer good for anything, except to be thrown out and trampled by men. You are the light of the world. A city on a hill cannot be hidden. Neither do people light a lamp and put it under a bowl. Instead they put it on its stand, and it gives light to everyone in the house. In the same way, let your light shine before men, that they may see your good deeds and praise your Father in heaven. (Matthew 5:13-16)

Salt has three main functions: it enhances flavor, preserves food, and stimulates thirst. When it stops doing these things, it becomes ineffective. Instead of imitating others, God calls us to be salt. Our interactions should inspire a longing for more. Others should see wisdom and vitality in us that have lasting significance. Our lives should inspire a desire for good, reflected in our actions and attitudes. Our relationships should serve as a beacon, guiding others toward a deeper connection with God. None of these qualities can be achieved if we live, act, and reflect the culture around us. We must resist being shaped by the world. This transformation happens only through the "renewing of the mind."

The third step in discovering God's will involves renewing our minds: "But be transformed by the renewing of your mind. Then you will be able to test and approve what God's will is—his good, pleasing, and perfect will." (Romans 12:2) Our transformation starts with resisting the world's system while renewing our minds. Understanding God's will means viewing the world around us from His perspective. The mind is incredibly powerful and can lead to our transformation.

Paul selects the Greek word from which we derive the term "metamorphosis"; it describes the process of starting as a larva and transforming into a butterfly. This change is complete, resulting in a form that bears no resemblance to its original state. Paul explains this idea further in his letter to the Ephesians.

> You were taught, with regard to your former way of life, to put off your old self, which is being corrupted by its deceitful desires; to be made new in the attitude of your minds; and to put on the new self, created to be like God in true righteousness and holiness. (Ephesians 4:22-24)

When we are taken from Satan's dark domain to God's kingdom of light, a profound change occurs in our thinking. Our minds remain the same flawed minds we had before we believed, but the blindness to God's love and redemption is lifted. This allows us, for the first time, to truly see God for who He is. The renewing process begins. Renewing the mind is crucial for perceiving and understanding God's will.

A renewed mind brings us closer to God as He draws near to us. Avoiding conformity to the pattern of this evil age cannot succeed without understanding how God views the world. When mankind fell in the Garden of Eden, our minds became darkened. Although humanity initially had a personal relationship with God, it began to fade as we replaced the unseen God with what we can see around us. Charles Ryrie in *Balancing the Christian Life*, (pp. 38–41), reminds us that without Christ, man's mind cannot understand the things of God.

> The mind of the unsaved person is not described in very flattering terms in the Scriptures. It is evil (Gen. 6:5); it is reprobate (Rom. 1:28). This is due to the rejection of the light of revelation which God gives to all men in nature (Rom. 1:18–21). In other words, it is self-determined reprobation brought on by man's willful rejection of what he could know of the power of God through the universal revelation of God in the creation. The unsaved man because of the Fall is without a critical faculty (Rom. 3:11) when it comes to understanding the things of God. This is not to say that he is without understanding or intelligence, but it is to say that his mind is darkened and vain (Eph. 4:17–18). Actually, it is at war with God (Rom. 8:6–7). It is defiled (literally, dyed with another color, Titus 1:15) and corrupt (1 Tim. 6:5). All of this is due to the fact that Satan has "blinded the minds of the unbelieving, that they might not see the light of the gospel of the glory of Christ, who is the image of God" (2 Cor. 4:4).

As we move from darkness into His light, we still struggle with the old mindset that tries to keep control. When this mindset aligns with the surrounding culture, our lives reveal to those who have never truly known Jesus. There are only two groups in this world: God's children and those of Satan. Believers face the challenge of shifting their mindset from that of enemies of God to that of His children. Without renewing the mind, God's will stays a mystery.

The renewal of the mind is an active and continuous process

rooted in understanding His Word and empowered by the Spirit of God. We have received the mind of Christ—a new way of thinking. The battle with this culture begins in the mind. Nielsen's research shows that U.S. adults spend an average of 11 hours a day consuming media across various platforms. These platforms promote philosophies that oppose God's will. The more our minds dwell on these influences, the more we may be drawn back into embracing thoughts and beliefs that reflect who we were before we came to know Christ. Focusing on the philosophies of our culture puts us in opposition to God's enemies, whose destinies lead to destruction, as they worship pleasure and boast about things they should feel shame for, all while setting their minds on "earthly things" (Philippians 3:19). In contrast, believers must set their minds on "things above, not on earthly things," because we have died to these ways and are alive only in Christ (Colossians 3:1-4). Many may think that believers live according to the standards of this world, but Paul reminds us that

> For though we live in the world, we do not wage war as the world does. The weapons we fight with are not the weapons of the world. On the contrary, they have divine power to demolish strongholds. We demolish arguments and every pretension that sets itself up against the knowledge of God, and we take captive every thought to make it obedient to Christ. (2 Corinthians 10:2-5)

By renewing our minds, we not only view our culture from God's perspective but also, through the Spirit, begin to see everything through the mind of Christ (1 Corinthians 2:16; Philippians 2:1-5). We start thinking positively (Philippians 4:8). Renewing our minds involves perceiving life through God's lens. Learning this perspective is only possible by developing habits that allow the Holy Spirit to guide our thoughts and lives. The mind is renewed by establishing routines that the Holy Spirit can use to transform our thinking. The athlete reminds us of the importance of being transformed through changes in our daily routines.

I have never been an athlete, but I know a few. Paul effectively compared living the Christian life to that of an athlete in competition.

Do you not know that in a race all the runners run, but only one gets the prize? Run in such a way as to get the prize. Everyone who competes in the games goes into strict training. They do it to get a crown that will not last; but we do it to get a crown that will last forever. Therefore I do not run like a man running aimlessly; I do not fight like a man beating the air. No, I beat my body and make it my slave so that after I have preached to others, I myself will not be disqualified for the prize. (1 Corinthians 9:24–27)

Too often, we believe that all the work is finished at salvation. We think, "Now that I am a child of God, everything is done, and I can rest and enjoy the ride." Paul would disagree. He believed that being a believer requires the mindset of an athlete. An athlete's success depends on a training program that best prepares them to win the race. Their daily routine reflects their goal of becoming a winning athlete. It includes what and when they eat, how they exercise, and how they mentally approach the sport. Their lives are turned upside down as they train to excel in their sport. Paul suggests that every believer should adopt a routine to improve their success as God's children. This is not legalism; these practices don't make us more saved; they become the foundation for renewing our minds so that we grow in our relationship with God each day.

Reflect & Respond

As you finish this chapter, take a few quiet moments to reflect on what God might be speaking to your heart. These questions help you remember key truths, deepen your understanding, challenge your assumptions, and motivate you to action. Whether you're working through them alone or with a group, invite the Holy Spirit to guide your thoughts, encourage honest conversations, and reveal the next step in your walk with Christ.

Let this be not just a review but a response of faith, obedience, and transformation.

1. According to James 4:4 and 1 Peter 2:9-12, what is the believer's relationship with the world, and how does friendship with the world impact our fellowship with God?

2. What are the three essential benefits of salt mentioned in Matthew 5:13, and how do they illustrate the influence and responsibility of Christians in the world?

3. How does the metaphor of "renewing of the mind" in Romans 12:2 connect to Paul's teaching in Ephesians 4:22-24 regarding putting off the old self and putting on the new self?

4. What challenges does American culture present to believers who resist conformity and maintain a renewed, transformed mind?

5. How does Paul's analogy of an athlete in 1 Corinthians 9:24-27 inspire spiritual discipline, and what lessons can believers learn for pursuing growth and godliness?

CHAPTER SEVEN

DEVELOPING THE HABITS
OF A PLEASING LIFE

*Spiritual disciplines are not about earning God's favor,
but aligning our hearts with His purposes.*
Richard Foster.

Throughout scripture, the presence or absence of spiritual habits separates those who please God from those who do not. Our minds are transformed through practicing habits that draw us closer to God and His will for our lives. Without these habits, renewal stops. Scripture reminds us that life is a journey we walk. Too often, in the Christian life, we take a passive approach, hoping it will lead to pleasing God. We read scripture and pray, hoping the Holy Spirit will inspire us to take actions that honor God. Living passively in the Christian life is like needing a job; instead of actively seeking one, we pray for a miracle, hoping that a miraculous God will drop a job into our laps. I wish that method worked, but it doesn't. To find a job, we must make it our goal. After searching all day, we can pray for God's blessing on our efforts.

Just as finding a job takes intentional effort, so does pleasing God. When we adopt spiritual practices or habits into our lives, we draw closer to God and His goodness. These spiritual practices, like the skills needed to build and maintain relationships, help us establish a connection with God that not only pleases Him but also transforms us. By practicing these habits, we renew our minds, and God uses them to bring about change. Each day, we grow nearer to Him, becoming more like Jesus and viewing the world through His eyes.

Several important points about these habits are necessary at this stage. They do not act as a blueprint for salvation or success. Practicing them paves the way to a closer relationship with God and His plan for your life. These habits are key to building a meaningful connection with our Creator. God is a person. To please Him, understanding Him is essential. He has a purpose, a way of doing things, a perspective, and a set of non-negotiables. These practices help us understand God's character more deeply than we could otherwise. God promises to reward anyone who approaches Him in faith and sincerely seeks Him (Hebrews 11:6). Our perceptions and thoughts can transform not only our minds but also our lives. Our lives improve when we develop these habits. Practicing and encouraging them will help us live the life we've always desired. When these habits become part of our daily routine, we begin to see our culture through God's eyes, leading to a renewed mindset.

You might wonder why I refer to these practices as habits rather than "spiritual disciplines." I avoid using the term "spiritual disciplines" because many of us have mentally separated the idea of spiritual disciplines from our physical activities. In church culture, we often distinguish the spiritual from the physical, even though they are connected. Spiritual claims should always be reflected in our actions. James, the brother of Jesus, wrote his letter with this concern in mind, among others. He reminds us of the practical side of faith. Speaking of Abraham, James writes,

> *You see that his faith and his actions were working together, and his faith was made complete by what he did... You see that a person is justified by what he does and not by faith alone. (James 2:22, 24)*

Humans tend to assign meanings to things without putting them into practice. James teaches that theory is worthless without action. You don't truly subscribe to a belief unless you also act on it. This truth may explain why Paul, in Romans 12:1, urges us to dedicate our bodies. He is not asking us to commit our lives as sacrifices. Nor is he commanding that we dedicate our minds and actions to Him. Since our bodies include our thoughts, beliefs, emotions, and identities, others can only recognize our commitment through our actions. Spiritual disciplines suggest that what happens is a mental activity that might not be visible in our habits. Spiritual habits or practices are expressions of what we do.

Habits also differ from spiritual disciplines in another way. Spiritual disciplines refer to activities performed as mental or spiritual practices. Only someone with a deep understanding of the term recognizes that it must include a physical habit. The renewing of the mind is not just mental exercises; it is the process of transforming how we think, perceive, and act. Dallas Willard often discussed spiritual transformation as something that isn't achieved just by stopping bad habits but by purposefully replacing them with new, grace-filled habits that connect us with God. In the broader context, Willard explains that transformation isn't about stopping sin through sheer effort but about training ourselves in new habits (spiritual disciplines) that gradually reshape our character to reflect Christ. "We cannot simply remove the old habit patterns, but must replace them with new ones that are strong and capable of directing our lives in God." (Dallas Willard, The Spirit of the Disciplines) Only by aligning our thoughts with God's can we truly please Him. These habits clarify why prayer, fellowship, service, and studying the Word are so vital. They are not meant to be "busy work," but serve as tools for renewing our minds so that our transformation remains ongoing and complete. They also illustrate Paul's admonition to "work out our salvation with fear and trembling" (Philippians 2:12).

These habits are not listed in any specific order of importance. They are like ingredients used to bake a cake, with each element helping to create a life that brings a smile to God's face. As readers encounter each essential habit, they should begin to add the related practices into their lives. These practices are the threads that weave the fabric of our Christian life. Everything starts with choosing the right path.

When we discover God's will for our lives and begin developing the habits of a healthy walk with the Lord, we experience a life full of impact, power, and gratitude as we deepen our relationship with Him. We learn to walk with God as our new habits renew our thinking.

The word "walk" is a compelling metaphor used in scripture to depict the daily life of a child of God. These verses highlight God's guidance, wisdom in His word, and the importance of following His path. The Greek word peripateo means "to walk" or "to conduct oneself." It is often used in the New Testament, usually in a metaphorical sense, to describe how someone lives or behaves. The NIV frequently translates this word as "live," capturing the whole meaning of the metaphor (Ephesians 5:2, Galatians 5:16, Colossians 1:10, 2 Corinthians 5:7, Ephesians 4:11, John 1:7, & Romans 6:4).

The symbolic use of "walking" in the Christian faith emphasizes how believers should live their lives. Scripture presents this walk as a fundamental part of the Christian journey. It is considered normal not because it mirrors the lives of most believers, but because it is the life that God has empowered us to live. We must be careful not to confuse normality with being ordinary or average. An explanation is needed at this point.

When I started my career in Medical Technology, much of the research focused on the causes of heart disease. Studies showed a link between heart disease and cholesterol. Once cholesterol testing became available in hospital labs, cardiologists began ordering it for their patients. This increased demand prompted us to offer the test to our medical staff. Our first step was to determine the normal cholesterol levels. With patient permission, we began taking an extra blood sample from each patient we treated. Within a few months, we tested thousands of samples and established the "normal" levels for our community. Our normal cholesterol range was from the mid-200s to the mid-300s mg/dL. After consulting with our cardiologist, we realized our normal levels were too high. Research showed that an ideal level for heart health was below 200 mg/dL. Our elevated "normal" values reflected our community, which explained the high rate of heart disease. The normal cholesterol level for our community was much higher than what it should have been physiologically. Our prosperous community had developed a lifestyle that was harming it. We had mistaken what is typical or average for what is healthy and normal. Similarly, Christians often confuse normal behavior with biblical behavior.

Many behaviors exhibited by today's believers might seem biblically normal, but they are ordinary or average, just like our initial cholesterol levels. They don't live spiritually healthy lifestyles that reflect Jesus and the teachings of the Word. Studies show that the surrounding secular culture influences the typical believer. Many believers spend their time chasing the American dream, mistakenly thinking that because they "accepted Jesus as their Savior," they are free to pursue the American version of happiness. They do not engage in the practices essential for nurturing a life that pleases the Lord. Without these habits, we risk becoming religious individuals who know about God but are never transformed by the renewing of the mind. In doing so, we miss the transformative life changes that come from intimately knowing Him.

To please God, our behavior must align with biblical standards. Our first steps to resist the world, renew our minds, and live in a way that shows God's will and pleases Him begin with developing healthy habits—habits that Scripture considers normal. Paul uses the metaphor of changing clothes to describe the process of replacing old habits with new ones.

Therefore, as God's chosen people, holy and dearly loved, clothe yourselves with compassion, kindness, humility, gentleness and patience. Bear with each other and forgive whatever grievances you may have against one another. Forgive as the Lord forgave you. And over all these virtues put on love, which binds them all together in perfect unity. (Colossians 3:12-14)

Forming a helpful mental image of integrating these habits into our lives requires an understanding of how medicine works.

Taking the Medicine

Cultivating transformative habits shields us from being shaped by the world while renewing our thoughts and perceptions of life. Developing these spiritual practices acts as a remedy that promotes spiritual health and lays the foundation for discovering God's will and pleasing Him. These habits improve a believer's overall well-being. Their consistent practice encourages a life that delights the Lord and reflects the life we have always desired. The challenge is that many people fail to see their need for this remedy. Sadly, it often takes a wake-up call before we admit our need for healing support.

I recall walking into a local pharmacy and noticing they had a blood pressure machine available for anyone to check their blood pressure. I sat down, slipped my arm into the opening, and pushed the button. The machine started hissing and inflating the cuff on my arm. As the cuff slowly released, a number flashed on the screen: 172/98. Wow, I thought. The machine must be broken. I probably don't have high blood pressure! Several days later, I returned to the machine and saw the same results.

A week later, after my wife urged me, I sat in my doctor's office with my arm in a blood pressure cuff again. My blood pressure was still high. The doctor prescribed medication to lower it, along with some lifestyle changes. After several weeks, my blood pressure went down to 110/70. I believed the change was due to my diet and exercise adjustments, so I stopped taking the medication. I thought losing a few pounds would fix the problem. During the first week, my BP stayed normal. By the end of the second week, it was creeping up but still within the normal range. By week three, it was 170/100. Yikes, I must have high blood pressure! I immediately restarted my medication, but my BP remained high for days before slowly returning to normal. Just like my blood pressure medication, our habits of renewing our minds need to be integrated into our lives instead of being isolated behaviors separated by weeks or months.

When I stopped taking the medicine, my blood pressure didn't rise immediately. It took time for the medicine to clear out of my system and lose its effectiveness. When we stop spending time in the Word, praying, serving, and fellowshipping, nothing changes right away. But over time, we start to feel a distance from ourselves and from God's family. When a crisis strikes and we suddenly realize we need the medicine, we pray, attend church, read our Bible, and volunteer, yet that perceived distance still remains. It's only after reestablishing this medicine as a regular habit that we begin to experience peace with our circumstances and feel God's presence.

Every believer needs this medicine. It is a mixture of ingredients that, when combined, the Holy Spirit uses to promote spiritual health in us as our minds are renewed. Taking this medicine strengthens us to resist reflecting the culture we live in. These habits work together in a believer's life to foster spiritual well-being. I believe this is what Paul implies when he reminds Timothy to,

> Be diligent in these matters: give yourself wholly to them, so that everyone may see your progress. Watch your life and doctrine closely. Persevere in them, because if you do, you will save both yourself and your hearers. (1 Timothy 4:15-16)

Being obedient to Paul requires consistency. The word "consistent" can be intimidating if you're wired like me. In terms of Myers-Briggs, I strongly identify as a Perceiving (P) type. I thrive on flexibility, spontaneity, and adaptability, preferring to keep my options open. In healthcare, I enjoyed being "on-call" because I liked responding to situations as they arose. A daily routine can feel too constricting for me. If you're like me, you might see "consistent" as impossible. While doing something once every few months doesn't count as regular, doing it a few times a week is a good start. For example, if you aim to read the Word daily, you might struggle and eventually give up, blaming yourself for another scheduling failure. Starting with a manageable schedule of several times a week is more likely to lead to success. Over time, once the habit is formed, you can increase its frequency. (I included a section in the Appendix derived from ChatGPT outlining the development of healthy habits.) If you identify as a Judging (J) type in Myers-Briggs, you probably embrace the idea of "consistent."

People with a judging preference tend to prefer structure, planning, and organization. They like sticking to a schedule and value a neat, settled life. This indicates they seek consistency and often resist changing their plans when disruptions happen. They are more likely to succeed in creating a daily routine. However, their challenge may be the temptation to focus on daily habits rather than the reasons behind them.

Twelve areas where habits need to be developed include time in the Word, in prayer, in fellowship at church, in service, in sharing our faith, in worship, in fasting, in confession, in resting, in giving, in solitude, and stewardship. Before discussing these habits, I need to address a growing tension that I know you must feel. You might wonder, "How will I add these many habits to my busy schedule?" Each of these habits is not performed daily; spending time fasting or practicing solitude may occur only a few times a year. Others, like praying, reading the Word, and worshiping, often happen together. Successfully applying these habits won't require 10 hours a day! (I have included a summary toward the end of this chapter that suggests the amount of time it takes to practice each habit.)

Habit one: Spending quality time in the Bible and meditation.

Your word is a lamp to my feet and a light for my path.
(Psalm 119:105)

In my younger years, I was an avid backpacker. For fifteen years, a friend and I explored most of Northern California's wilderness areas and national parks. Heading out on a trail in Yosemite National Park often started from Yosemite Valley. Our first two hours involved walking on narrow paths ascending from the valley floor in complete darkness. Flashlights lit up a narrow trail along a cliff that dropped several thousand feet on one side, while the other side featured a vertical cliff. When I read Psalm 119:105, I remember those trips. We needed a lamp to see each step, which also lit the path ahead. The Bible is God's light, guiding every step of our lives while revealing our immediate steps and the direction of the path before us.

Discerning God's path for our lives is impossible without the Bible. The Psalmist in Psalm 19 reminds us that creation reveals the presence of a Creator, but without the special revelation found in the Bible, we cannot know anything specific about Him or His plan for our lives. Studying the Bible is essential for understanding our lives from God's perspective. However, as we begin this study, we must be cautious not to see the accumulation of knowledge as the goal. We aim to apply what we learn. James argues in his letter that we should live out what we read.

> Do not merely listen to the word, and so deceive yourselves. Do what it says. Anyone who listens to the word but does not do what it says is like a man who looks at his face in a mirror and, after looking at himself, goes away and immediately forgets what he looks like. But the man who looks intently into the perfect law that gives freedom, and continues to do this, not forgetting what he has heard, but doing it—he will be blessed in what he does. (James 2:22-25)

James's main point is that faith without deeds is dead. In other words, simply believing without acting isn't true belief. We need to be careful not to confuse time spent in the Word with morning devotions or just a quick read of Scripture. These activities can meet the time requirement for the Word, but for many, they become obligatory duties forced by Christian culture. Many read a passage each morning and start their day feeling guilt-free. If asked if they spend time in the Word daily, they can say "yes" without guilt. Others study and understand the Word thoroughly; they might analyze the verbs and check cross-references. If they enjoy scholarly pursuits, they compare each passage with others to understand the overall message.

Although both approaches produce results, neither captures the true importance of regularly spending quality time with the Bible. When we stand before the Lord, we won't be praised for the time spent in the Word or the amount of Scripture we understand. Instead, we'll be accountable for how we apply what we've read. The Lord values obedience over merely possessing knowledge. He isn't impressed by how much time we dedicate to reading or studying the Bible. The time invested and the knowledge gained are only means for application and transformation. The teachings of 2 Timothy and Hebrews show that the Bible is a living agent of change. Scripture, inspired by God, effectively reveals the core issues. With the living Word, nothing is hidden from God.

All Scripture is God-breathed and is useful for teaching, rebuking, correcting and training in righteousness, so that the man [or woman – my addition] of God may be thoroughly equipped for every good work. (2 Timothy 3:16)

For the word of God is living and active. Sharper than any double-edged sword, it penetrates even to dividing soul and spirit, joints and marrow; it judges the thoughts and attitudes of the heart. Nothing in all creation is hidden from God's sight. Everything is uncovered and laid bare before the eyes of him to whom we must give account. (Hebrews 4:12-13)

When we apply the Word to our lives, the Holy Spirit works diligently to shape us into the image of the Son of God.

And we, who with unveiled faces all reflect the Lord's glory, are being transformed into his likeness with ever-increasing glory, which comes from the Lord, who is the Spirit. (2 Corinthians 3:18)

Reading the Bible this way transforms our lives. We build a relationship with the author as He touches our hearts and minds, cleansing us. A believer can never attain spiritual health without the cleansing power of the Word. Not only do we become capable and fully useful, but we also grow in godliness.

Paul reminded Timothy as he pastored the Ephesian church.

Have nothing to do with godless myths and old wives' tales; rather, train yourself to be godly. For physical training is of some value, but godliness has value for all things, holding promise for both the present life and the life to come. (1 Timothy 4:7-8)

The idea of godliness has been overshadowed in today's culture. For many, revering God feels unfamiliar. We have become too casual with God and forgotten that He is still a consuming fire (Hebrews 12:29). Some of us are more worried about our physical health and appearance than about our decreasing concern for godliness. Yet, godliness is much more beneficial. I am not saying that we should neglect our efforts to stay physically healthy. We need to exercise and take care of our physical health, but not at the cost of becoming godly.

For years, LouAnna and I jogged together. We ran a couple of miles every weekday and an extra mile on Saturdays. We also belonged to a health club where we played racquetball. I was in better health than I had been in years. Never mind the fact that my spiritual life was non-existent. While I could exercise the discipline to care for my body, I couldn't find the time to cultivate godliness. Spending time in the Bible and applying its truths to my life was something I did sporadically, and it showed in my attitude. However, when I became as serious about being in the Word as I was about jogging, my life began to turn around. My life started to reflect Christ more, and I developed a growing reverence for God. Paul understood this when he reminded Titus in the introduction to the letter he sent.

Paul, a servant of God and an apostle of Jesus Christ for the faith of God's elect and the knowledge of the truth that leads to godliness. (Titus 1:1)

Paul uses "epiginosko" when speaking of knowledge. This type of knowledge promotes godliness. A structured approach is essential for a deep understanding of the Bible. Here are ten steps to help you get the most out of your Bible reading.

1. Pray for understanding. Ask the Holy Spirit to guide you (John 16:13). Gaining spiritual insight is crucial for understanding the truth of God's Word.

2. Choose a reliable translation and keep a record. Use an accurate and easy-to-read translation, such as the ESV, NASB, NIV, or NKJV. Avoid paraphrasing for deeper study. Keeping a written record of your time in the Word is helpful as you document the passage and your understanding of it.

3. Read the passage in context. Never isolate a verse. Review the surrounding passages to grasp the whole meaning. Consider the chapter, book, and overall biblical narrative while you read.

4. Identify the genre. Genre refers to a category or type of literature, art, music, or other forms of expression that share common characteristics in form, style, or subject matter. Different genres—such as history, poetry, prophecy, and epistles—require distinct approaches. Psalms are poetic, while Paul's letters are instructional.

5. Compare Scripture to Scripture. The Bible interprets itself. Use cross-references to understand how different passages connect.

6. Study key words and phrases, looking up essential terms

in their original Hebrew or Greek meanings. Tools like Strong's Concordance can be helpful.

7. Understand the historical and cultural context. The Bible was written in a different time and culture. Study the customs, audience, and historical background. Many Bibles, especially "study" Bibles, include detailed introductions that help readers understand the historical and cultural setting.

8. Ask key questions while reading. In "Living By the Book," by Howard G. and William D. Hendricks, the authors suggest that Bible study should begin with three questions.

   - Observation: As I read the passage, what do I observe?
   - Interpretation: What does the passage mean?
   - Application: How do I apply it to my life?

9. Utilize practical study tools. Commentaries, Bible dictionaries, and study Bibles can offer deeper insights. Exercise discernment with your sources. (See a list of resources in the Appendix.)

10. Apply the Word to Your Life. James 1:22 urges us to be doers, not just hearers. Look for ways to put the truth you've learned into practice. My writing partner, Dr. Marty Trammell, has spent over thirty years journaling in the Word daily. Not only has he built up a wealth of Bible knowledge, but his life also reflects the Jesus he serves. He also gauges his growth by re-reading previous entries. Being in the Word naturally goes with prayer, and we often find ourselves reading, praising, and praying all at once.

Habit Two: Spend regular and consistent time in prayer.

Rejoice in the Lord always. I will say it again: Rejoice! Let your gentleness be evident to all. The Lord is near. Do not be anxious about anything, but in everything, by prayer and petition, with thanksgiving, present your requests to God. And the peace of God, which transcends all understanding, will guard your hearts and minds in Christ Jesus. (Philippians 4:4-7)

One of the quickest ways to make today's believer feel guilty is to ask how much they pray. Even those who pray often feel it is never enough. I had the privilege of pastoring alongside Dr. Phillip Howard, who founded Valley Bible Church in Hercules, California, in 1971. He is one of the few people I know who dedicates much of his morning to prayer. However, when asked, he would admit that he still feels guilty about not praying enough. In an interview, Billy Graham confessed that he would pray more if he had the chance to do it all over again. I have never met a man or woman who believes they pray enough.

In fifty years of ministry, I have met many who don't pray. Most believers spend little time in prayer. We tend to pray only when necessary, during a crisis, or after failing to solve a problem. We overlook the importance of Paul's reminder to the church at Thessalonica to "pray without ceasing.

Believers who make a difference are people of prayer. This was true for David, Joseph, Abraham, Paul, Jesus, Daniel, Nehemiah, and many others. They understood that prayer is more than just asking for things; it involves being in God's presence and sharing a close, personal moment with Him. This time is a special gift given to God's children. Christianity isn't just a religion; it's a relationship with the living God of the Bible. Nowhere is this relationship clearer than when we are welcomed into the throne room to spend time with Him. It is personal, genuine, and vulnerable. We share our problems with the One who created the universe. In prayer, God moves heaven and earth to respond to us. Listening to a Q & A with Pastor Jack Hayford, he was asked,

"If God is all-powerful and all-knowing, why do we pray?"

"We pray," he responded, "because God has reserved some things that He wants accomplished but will not do unless we ask." All the saints in the Bible understood this truth. While Daniel was praying, the angel Gabriel arrived with the message, "As soon as you began to pray, an answer was given, which I have come to tell you..." (Daniel 9:23). Later, Daniel is reminded that because he demonstrated the prerequisites of prayer, God answered him. The angel said, "Since the first day that you set your mind to gain understanding and to humble yourself before your God, your words were heard, and I have come in response to them." (Daniel 10:11). He was determined to understand God and humble himself before Him. God saw his heart (as He sees ours) and responded. When we pray earnestly, our prayer life begins to reflect the relational nature of conversing with a loving father who desires what is best for us and everyone for whom we pray.

Speaking of prayer, Leonard Sweet explains this spiritual calling of the soul in Learn to Dance the Soul Salsa. (Pages 35-36)

> Our direct uplink (or better, surroundlink) to the Almighty is called *prayer*. Prayer is the primal and primary religious act. Prayer is the trigger mechanism that releases God's will in our life and world. Prayer is the art of hole-punching the sky so that 'as it is in heaven' becomes an earthly reality. As with all high-powered voltage sources, prayer mandates certain vectors. (page 35)

He continues to outline the vectors of prayer.
The first prayer vector is to change your posture when you pray.
The second prayer vector is be prepared to be changed.
The third prayer vector is that each of us will pray differently.
The fourth prayer vector is to pray without ceasing.
The fifth prayer vector is to make all of life a prayer vector.

When we pray regularly, we take essential medicine for our spiritual health. It also reminds us that God answers our prayers.

For years, the Rollins family kept a prayer journal. As we prayed, we recorded our requests. Later, when God answered, we documented those answers in the journal. In the early 1980s, the college where we served faced financial struggles. As funding for the school decreased, we went without paychecks. Often, our prayers centered on basic needs. One time, we prayed for a utility bill of $127. We didn't have enough money to pay it. We could have asked our parents or friends for help, but instead, we turned to the Lord. We wrote in our journal, "Praying for God to provide money for a $127 utility bill.

Later that week, a pastor called to ask for a favor. He had organized a couples' retreat for his church, scheduled to start in a few days. However, his speaker had just told him that he was sick with the flu.

"Would you come and lead our retreat?" I could hear the desperation in his voice.

Two days later, we reached the church and spent the weekend discussing biblical principles for a successful marriage. When we returned home at the end of the week, God blessed us with more than the $127 we had asked for in our prayer journal.

Over the years, we often revisited the journal pages that held the answers to our prayers. Each time we faced scarcity, we turned to our journals to remember God's faithfulness. If we do not document our prayers, we risk losing track of our requests and forgetting God's responses. Those answers are crucial because the enemy will try to convince us that God has abandoned us. When discouragement begins to creep into our thoughts, a quick review of our prayer journal reminds us of God's faithfulness. The Psalms often serve as a record of the psalmist's prayer journal.

The Psalms are full of times when the psalmist recognizes God's faithfulness in answering prayers. These prayers often show deep feelings, from anguish and despair to joy and thanks. Here are a few examples of how the psalmists acknowledged God's response to their prayers.

I sought the Lord, and he answered me; he delivered me from all my fears. (Psalm 34:4)

The Lord has heard my cry for mercy; the Lord accepts my prayer. (Psalm 6:9)

When hard pressed, I cried to the Lord; he brought me into a spacious place. The Lord is with me; I will not be afraid. (Psalm 118:5-6)

In my distress I called to the Lord; I cried to my God for help. From his temple he heard my voice; my cry came before him, into his ears. (Psalm 18:6)

I waited patiently for the Lord; he turned to me and heard my cry. He lifted me out of the slimy pit, out of the mud and mire; he set my feet on a rock and gave me a firm place to stand. (Psalm 40:1-2)

The Psalmist recorded the answers to his prayers, serving as a reminder of God's faithfulness in responding to us. Throughout the Psalms, a recurring theme is that God hears and acts on behalf of His people. These prayers reveal the psalmists' intimate relationship with God, expressing their struggles and confidence in His response. They also encourage believers today to seek God's help in times of need, trusting that He listens and will respond according to His timing and wisdom.

The medicine's first two ingredients are time spent in the Word and time devoted to prayer. The third ingredient is quality time with God's family.

Habit Three: Fellowship in the Church - Strengthening the Body of Christ

Fellowship is a vital part of the Christian life. It goes beyond just socializing; it embodies a deep spiritual bond among believers centered on Christ, fostering encouragement, accountability, and growth. Coming together strengthens our faith, deepens our love for each other, and prepares us to carry out God's purpose.

Over twenty times in the New Testament, we are encouraged

to connect with fellow believers. We are called to uplift, correct, love, forgive, confess to, bear, pray for, meet with, serve, show kindness, display compassion, and worship together. Scripture teaches us that we cannot thrive alone. We need each other. I cannot succeed without you, and you cannot succeed without me. Our culture promotes isolation — a world of drive-up windows and automatic garage doors. We can order a meal without ever leaving our homes. It's so easy to isolate, but Scripture calls us to fellowship.

The Bible emphasizes the importance of believers gathering together to encourage and support one another.

> *Not neglecting to meet together, as is the habit of some, but encouraging one another, and all the more as you see the Day drawing near. (Hebrews 10:25)*

This verse emphasizes three essential aspects of Christian fellowship:

- Consistency – Meeting regularly with fellow believers.
- Encouragement – Supporting each other in faith and perseverance.
- Urgency – As Christ's return approaches, our need for unity and strength grows.

Christian fellowship is crucial for spiritual growth and perseverance. Paul reminds us that a vital part of our stability and maturity occurs when we are united.

> *It was he who gave some to be apostles, some to be prophets, some to be evangelists, and some to be pastors and teachers, to prepare God's people for works of service, so that the body of Christ may be built up until we all reach unity in the faith and in the knowledge of the Son of God and become mature, attaining to the whole measure of the fullness of Christ. Then we will no longer be infants, tossed back and forth by the waves, and blown here and there by every wind of teaching and by the cunning and craftiness of men in their deceitful scheming. Instead, speaking*

the truth in love, we will in all things grow up into him who is the Head, that is, Christ. From him the whole body, joined and held together by every supporting ligament, grows and builds itself up in love, as each part does its work. (Eph 4:11-16)

Being together under the guidance and teaching of gifted individuals fosters maturity and stability in our lives. Many younger believers think they can be saved without joining a church community. The flaw in this belief is clear in this passage. God has designed the church to be a primary source of our growth, stability, and maturity. Without the church, a believer's development is hindered. However, growth is not the only benefit we gain from being together.

During our time together, our faith is strengthened through each other's company. In a world filled with challenges, believers encourage and remind one another of God's promises (1 Thessalonians 5:11). We find accountability and support within the community. The church is called to carry one another's burdens (Galatians 6:2). Serving within the church has a profound impact on us. Paul confirms this in his letter to the Ephesians, where he states that the role of a leader is to equip believers for service. Every believer possesses unique gifts to strengthen the church (1 Peter 4:10). Scripture provides a model of the early church.

The early church demonstrated a strong sense of fellowship.

And they devoted themselves to the apostles' teaching and the fellowship, to the breaking of bread and the prayers. (Acts 2:42)

This verse outlines five pillars of early Christian fellowship:

1. Learning together - growing in faith through biblical teaching.
2. Sharing life - meeting each other's needs.
3. Breaking bread involves sharing meals and engaging in communion together.
4. Praying together means coming together as a community to seek God.

5. Serving one another through the use of our spiritual gifts.

The early church believers recognized that Gatherings were essential, not optional, and that remains true today.

There is a growing belief among many that being affiliated with the "church" is not essential to living the Christian life. Many individuals have either experienced "church hurt" or have read about it and concluded that church involvement is unnecessary for the Christian. They overlook that God designed the church to be a key part of attaining maturity in our lives. Paul suggests in Ephesians 4:11-16 that without involvement in a local church, we remain unstable and are swayed by every false teaching. Without fellowship within the church, we cannot fully grow into the image of God's Son. Much of our growth begins with church attendance and participation, but doesn't end there.

Fellowship takes many forms, such as attending church services, participating in small groups or Bible studies, serving in ministry, praying for and with others, and mentoring those seeking friendship and growth. Fellowship is not optional; it is essential for a thriving Christian life and a renewed mind. God designed us to grow in community, support one another, and live out our faith together. By actively engaging in fellowship, we strengthen our faith, build lasting relationships, and glorify God as one body in Christ. Typically, our opportunities to serve begin through fellowship in a local church.

Habit Four: Service - Living Out Christ's Love

Peter is quick to remind us about serving when he writes:

Each one should use whatever gift he has received to serve others, faithfully administering God's grace in its various forms. If anyone speaks, he should do it as one speaking the very words of God. If anyone serves, he should do it with the strength God provides, so that in all things God may be praised through Jesus Christ. To him be the glory and the power for ever and ever.

Amen. (1 Peter 4:10-11)

Service is a core expression of the Christian faith. We are gifted to serve, offering a way to reflect Christ's love, humility, and compassion through our time, talents, and resources in aiding others. Serving others is not just an act of charity; it is a calling and a way of life for those who follow Jesus. Service gives us purpose and influences the lives of others. The Bible teaches that serving is not optional but a duty for believers.

You, my brothers and sisters, were called to be free. But do not use your freedom to indulge the flesh; rather, serve one another humbly in love. (Galatians 5:13)

Paul emphasizes three key aspects of Christian service:

1. It is a calling – We are set free to serve, not just to focus on ourselves.
2. It requires humility – True service is done with a heart of love, not for recognition.
3. It expresses love – Serving others demonstrates God's love in action.

Service is vital for Christian growth and witness; it reflects Christ's example. Jesus came not to be served but to serve (Mark 10:45). Every believer has gifts to strengthen the body of Christ (Ephesians 4:12), building up the Church. Jesus wants the Church to grow and stand as the pillar of truth. Growth will not occur unless each believer serves, and the Church's progress often depends on believers' willingness to serve others. Unbelievers see this demonstration of Christ's love and, as a result, become part of God's family. Serving brings joy and fulfillment while aligning our actions with God's purpose (Acts 20:35). Jesus demonstrated all of this by coming to serve.

Jesus demonstrated perfect service through His life, ministry, and ultimate sacrifice. One of the most powerful examples is when He washed His disciples' feet.

When he had finished washing their feet, he put on his clothes and returned to his place. 'Do you understand what I have done for you?' he asked them. 'You call me "Teacher" and "Lord," and rightly so, for that is what I am. Now that I, your Lord and Teacher, have washed your feet, you also should wash one another's feet. I have set you an example that you should do as I have done for you.' (John 13:12-15)

This act of humility teaches us that no task is too small or beneath us when serving others. It shows us how to serve and highlights the importance of accepting love from others. Most of us excel at giving but find it hard to accept. In this way, we mirror Peter, who first resisted having his feet washed. Jesus modeled the give-and-take of love, demonstrating both giving and receiving.

I have always valued Rick Warren's insights into how God designed us to serve. In my previous role as a pastor, we used a foundational program based on Rick Warren's work, which is outlined in the book, The Purpose Driven Church. Rick reminds us that we all have a SHAPE for service and ministry. SHAPE is an acronym for spiritual gifts, a heart for service, abilities to serve, a personality that makes serving more comfortable, and experiences—both painful and positive—that contribute to meaningful and impactful service opportunities. We are all shaped for ministry.

There are many ways to serve, both inside and outside the church. Genuine Christian service focuses on attitude rather than just actions. God wants a willing heart (2 Corinthians 9:7), a humble spirit (Philippians 2:3-4), and a selfless mindset that puts the needs of others before our own (1 Peter 4:10). Christian service shows love, humility, and obedience to God. It's not about seeking recognition but about glorifying Christ through our actions. Whether in the church, community, or daily life, every act of service is an opportunity to reflect God's love and bring His kingdom nearer.

Habit Five: Evangelism - Sharing the Good News of Jesus Christ

Evangelism is a core calling for every believer. It involves sharing the Gospel, the good news of Jesus Christ, with others so they may come to faith in Him. Evangelism is not just for pastors or missionaries; it is meant for all Christians who have experienced God's grace and salvation. Jesus' final command to His disciples, known as The Great Commission, is found in Matthew:

> Go therefore and make disciples of all nations, baptizing them in the name of the Father and of the Son and of the Holy Spirit, teaching them to observe all that I have commanded you. And behold, I am with you always, to the end of the age. (Matthew 28:19-20)

This passage highlights several important aspects of evangelism:

Go – Evangelism requires intentionality; we must act.

Make Disciples – It is more than just sharing the Gospel; it includes guiding others toward spiritual growth.

All Nations – The Gospel is for everyone, regardless of background.

Baptizing and Teaching – Evangelism leads to discipleship and commitment to Christ.

Jesus' Presence – We are not alone; Christ empowers us in this mission.

Many Christians hesitate to share the Gospel out of fear, doubt, or lack of knowledge. I grew up in a church culture that focused on evangelism, which involved memorizing a short version of the gospel and sharing it whenever possible with someone unchurched. It took me years to realize that, for me—and I believe for most of us—sharing the gospel "cold turkey" was ineffective. While working in healthcare, I found that sharing the gospel required earning the right to talk about it. Being a genuine believer helped me explain why I was who I was. Sharing the gospel became effective when I was seen as a sincere Christian. My message reached a wall when I acted hypocritically, which never truly touched the listener's soul.

As a pastor, I have noticed that many people are afraid to practice this habit. Most of these fears come from four areas: fear of rejection, uncertainty about what to say, anxiety about answering difficult questions about the Bible, and feeling unqualified because they are not pastors. The fear of rejection is probably the most common reason for not sharing the gospel.

I remember as a college student witnessing to my best friend. We grew up together and lived together during our first years in college. After getting married, we commuted 30 miles to college together until we graduated. During that time, we discussed all the world's problems, including those related to religion. He believed in God but thought that most religions served the same God under different names. We spent hours talking and debating our views. Over time, he could recite the gospel he had not yet accepted. In those rare moments at college when I was teased or mocked about my faith, he would defend me with what he knew about the gospel. We stayed friends after graduating, but we didn't discuss spiritual matters much as our lives began to diverge. He was in medical school, which left little time for socializing. One afternoon, while talking on the phone, I invited him to a revival meeting at our church, and he accepted. That night, he accepted Jesus as his Savior. It all started with friendship and many conversations over a decade before he responded to the Holy Spirit's work. It's a mistake to think that simply knowing and sharing the gospel abruptly with a stranger is the usual way to outreach. It might work for some, but not for most. Hearing and believing the good news is a process, not a one-time event. It's also best done by friends rather than strangers. Studies show that over 80% of believers were saved between ages 7 and 25 because a friend or family member shared their life and message. Sometimes, you only get to share your life and message without seeing immediate results. I've found this to be true many times.

While working in healthcare, I trained a young woman named Ellen (not her real name) to draw blood from patients. She worked as a phlebotomist for several years. I was on the lab's evening shift when I first met Ellen. My days were spent as a seminary student, and Ellen often saw me in the office working on assignments. Many times, she initiated conversations expressing her rejection of religion. A few years later, I left healthcare for an administrative position at a Northwest Christian college. As she entered her twenties, she left the hospital to work at one of the casinos in North Lake Tahoe. LouAnna and I tried to stay in touch. Eventually, I received a letter from her telling us that she had accepted Jesus as her Savior. We had planted seeds during our years working together, and God provided a neighbor in South Lake Tahoe who, in Ellen's words, "believed the same things that you believed." One late night, she walked down to their house, and they led her to the Lord. We should never let the fear of rejection keep us from being authentic Christians to those around us. As we develop friendships, natural opportunities to share our faith will arise. We should pray and look for them. The second reason people give for not sharing their faith is uncertainty about what to say.

The gospel is like an onion. On the surface, it seems to be a simple story. But when you peel back the first layer, you discover a deeper, more complex narrative. We might mistakenly think we can't say anything until we fully understand every part of the gospel story. The truth is, there are many ways to share the good news. The gospel is a beautifully wrapped truth that includes the redemptive story of the Bible. God created the universe and everything in it. He made man and woman to live in a garden on earth. They were perfect in their friendship with God, and their relationship was mutually satisfying. Their only rule was not to eat from the Tree of the Knowledge of Good and Evil. But they ate from the tree in their disobedience, and sin and death entered their lives. This sin affected and separated them from their previous close relationship with God.

This story is told in Genesis. Because of their disobedience, all their descendants inherit this sinful nature. The biblical story from Genesis to Matthew shows how God's plan of redemption unfolds. Matthew, Mark, Luke, and John introduce us to Jesus Christ, the center and solution of God's plan to offer salvation. From these four gospels, we learn that Jesus, who is God, came to give his body as a sacrifice for the sins of anyone who believes that he died for them. John 3:16-17, Romans 5:8, and Ephesians 2:8-10 teach us that salvation comes through Jesus' sacrifice. God accepted this sacrifice when He died on the cross, and His resurrection proved that God was pleased with it. When people believe this message, they accept Jesus as their savior, and a new life begins. The key is that the work of the Holy Spirit is vital when we share our faith. He convicts with the gospel and makes it clear. It's a miracle every time someone accepts Christ as their savior. Knowing what to say may not be enough for some of us to share the message.

Some of us hesitate to share because we fear being asked difficult questions about a Bible topic. Many years ago, a couple contacted my office to see if we could meet. I had just finished a teaching series on creation, and since I had never met the couple, I wondered what questions they might have taken from my sermons. I assumed they were believers wanting to explore the Genesis story more deeply.

As I sat with the couple, it became clear that neither was a believer. He was a biologist who dismissed the creation story, comparing the miracles in the Bible to Aesop's fables—storytelling mythology meant to teach a lesson. He saw Jesus as a good man whose disciples wrote about in glowing yet unrealistic terms. He did not believe Jesus was God; instead, he thought the New Testament writers deified him out of admiration and love for the man.

The couple presented a sheet of paper containing intricate scientific questions related to the creation story. I thought of Hebrews,

By faith we understand that the universe was formed at God's command, so that what is seen was not made out of what was visible. (Hebrews 11:3)

As I laid down the sheet of questions, I mentioned that even if I could answer every scientific question about the creation story, they would not believe me because our belief in the Bible is rooted in faith in God and His Son. "I am not suggesting that Christians accept the Bible narrative over scientific fact by blind, sometimes ignorant, faith. I am saying that it takes a work of God on our hearts to believe the Bible is the Word of God – free from error," I said.

"Are you saying that science is wrong about these things?" he asked.

"No, I am saying that we must first believe that the Bible is the Word of God and without error. That belief doesn't start with what the Bible says about creation; it begins with what it teaches about Jesus and who we are as God's creation. A person of faith who is also a scientist will spend their life harmonizing the truths of the Bible with the discoveries of science. But it all starts with asking who Jesus is and why he is important."

They were unhappy with my answer, yet they continued attending our services. A year later, they became believers. Subsequent conversations focused on aligning the teachings of the Bible with science. After their conversion, their questions about the Bible changed as faith became the lens through which they sought answers. We should never fear difficult questions. Reflecting on the list they initially gave me, I found that most were too challenging for me to answer as someone with a science background. My response to many of them still is, "I don't know." While reading this, you might have one lingering worry about sharing your testimony: you feel unqualified.

The disciples felt the same way. Many of them came from similar backgrounds and were seen as ordinary people. God uses average individuals to spread His message (1 Corinthians 1:26-27). One of the biggest misconceptions in many churches is the divide between clergy and laity. Many of us believe that only professionally trained pastors are the right people to evangelize. Every believer is called to share their faith when the opportunity presents itself. So, where do we begin?

In a recent conversation with Alex Absalom, co-author of "Discipleship that Fits," I was reminded that evangelism starts with prayer. We are surrounded by unchurched people at work, in our communities, and in various social settings. As we meet others, we should seek the Holy Spirit's guidance to identify those who might be open to the gospel. We should write their names on our prayer list and pray for them. In this step, we ask for opportunities and wisdom to share. Prayer invites the Holy Spirit to begin His work and softens our hearts toward them as we await answers to this prayer.

Meanwhile, we are getting ready to share what we will say. Evangelism is an important habit that fosters peace in our lives. Paul reminded Philemon of the importance of sharing our faith.

> I pray that you may be active in sharing your faith, so that you will have a full understanding of every good thing we have in Christ. (Philemon 6)

The phrase "full understanding" translates the Greek word *epiginosko,* which was mentioned in a previous chapter on knowledge. It indicates that a life without sharing our faith lacks the experiential knowledge of all the beneficial things we have in Christ.

Evangelism is a calling for every believer and a privilege to share the good news of Jesus Christ. Whether through conversations, lifestyle choices, or technology, we have countless opportunities to share His love. By stepping out in faith, we can engage in God's plan to bring salvation to the world. This is a vital practice, as renewing our minds transforms us. These five habits—time in the Word, prayer, fellowshipping with other believers, serving others, and sharing our faith—lead us to the sixth habit: worship.

Habit Six: Worshiping the God We Love

Many of us have reduced worship to just a time of singing in church before the sermon. We even call it "the worship service." However, worship is an attitude of giving worth to God, and it can (and should) happen almost anywhere. Worship is the heart's response to God's greatness, goodness, and glory. It involves love, reverence, and devotion, expressed both privately and publicly. True worship is not only an outward action but a deep spiritual connection with God that aligns our hearts with His will.

In John 4:24, Jesus taught that "God is spirit, and those who worship him must worship in spirit and truth." This means genuine worship is not limited to a specific place, ritual, or tradition. Instead, it flows from a heart transformed by the Holy Spirit and anchored in the truth of God's Word. It involves engaging our entire being in worship while allowing the Holy Spirit to guide and empower our love for God. Worshipping in spirit is not just about feelings; it's about a deep, personal relationship with God and His will (Romans 8:26). Worshiping in truth means authentic worship is based on knowing who God really is, as revealed in Scripture. It's not just about personal preferences or feelings but also about recognizing God's attributes, works, and promises (Psalm 145:18). The Bible and church tradition help us understand the different aspects of worship.

Private worship is a crucial part of a believer's life. It includes personal prayer, meditation on Scripture, singing, and praising God as we show our gratitude and love through music and hymns. It also involves a lifestyle that demonstrates obedience and honors God in everything we do. When we gather, we often take part in corporate worship with others.

As the Body of Christ unites, corporate worship brings believers together to glorify God and support one another in their faith. It includes congregational singing, preaching and teaching, praying together, giving, and celebrating the ordinances of baptism and communion.

Worship should be a way of life. It goes beyond church services or personal devotions. It should be reflected in our daily lives through:

- Obedience to God's will involves living a life that honors Him (1 Samuel 15:22).
- Loving others: Demonstrating God's love through service (Matthew 22:37-39).
- Gratitude in all circumstances – A heart that rejoices in God, even during trials (1 Thessalonians 5:16-18).
- Offering our talents and resources - using our gifts to glorify God (Colossians 3:23-24).

I remember many backpacking trips to the wilderness areas of the West Coast, where I felt profound worship while sitting by a lake or stream, breathing in God's creation. Sometimes, I was moved to tears. Worship goes beyond a song, a prayer, or a church service—it represents a lifestyle of devotion to God. Whether alone or with others, we worship the God we love by adoring Him, praising Him, and aligning our hearts with His truth. As we grow deeper in worship, we develop a closer connection with God and become more like Him, reflecting His glory to the world. Not only is He pleased with us, but we also begin to see the path He has set for us.

Habit Seven: Fasting - Drawing Near to God

Fasting is a spiritual practice where believers abstain from food or distractions to focus their hearts and minds on God. It is an act of humility, dependence, and devotion, seeking His presence, guidance, and strength. Fasting has become a new habit that has transformed my mind. It involves refraining from food and feasting on God's presence. It is a time to deepen our relationship with Him through prayer, worship, and reliance on His Word.

Jesus spoke about fasting, saying:

When you fast, do not look somber as the hypocrites do, for they disfigure their faces to show others they are fasting. Truly I tell you, they have received their reward in full. But when you fast, put oil on your head and wash your face, so that it will not be obvious to others that you are fasting, but only to your Father, who is unseen; and your Father, who sees what is done in secret, will reward you. (Matthew 6:16-18)

Fasting should be approached with sincerity, humility, and expectation—believing that God observes and responds.

Growing up in a conservative church, I was never exposed to fasting. I have only recently begun to understand the biblical reasons for its practice. Fasting is mentioned throughout Scripture for various purposes. The early church fasted before making important decisions (Acts 13:2-3) to seek God's guidance. In the Old Testament, fasting was often part of repentance and confession, as people responded to God's Word and turned away from sin (Joel 2:12, Jonah 3:5-10). Fasting served as a way for God's people to gain spiritual strength and renewal as they drew closer to Him (Isaiah 58:6-11). Daniel fasted while interceding for others (Daniel 9:3). Jesus fasted before beginning His public ministry (Matthew 4:1-2). As we consider the biblical narrative, we are reminded that removing ourselves from the distractions surrounding us is often necessary.

Sitting in a restaurant, I noticed a family of six at a table across the room. Five members were on their phones while the father read the newspaper. When the meal arrived, everyone ate without interrupting their time on their phones or newspapers. Most continued using their phones even while paying the bill and leaving. As I looked around the restaurant, I observed that about a third of the thirty seated patrons were on their phones. This made me realize we have a problem that fasting could help address. Fasting is not just about food.

There are various ways to fast, depending on personal beliefs, health, and spiritual needs. Many distractions surround us, pulling our attention away from the spiritually important parts of our lives. The complete fast in the Old Testament involved avoiding all food and drink except water for a specific period (Esther 4:16). Daniel opted for a partial fast, avoiding particular foods (Daniel 10:2-3). Today, a popular trend is intermittent fasting, where people fast for a set amount of time each day. Lastly, there is the non-food fast, where we avoid distractions like social media, entertainment, and other comforts to focus on God.

If you're new to fasting, consider these steps:
- Begin with a prayer, asking God to give you strength as you strive to draw closer to Him and understand His plans for your life.
- Clarify your fasting goals - What do you hope to accomplish? Spiritual renewal, guidance, or a breakthrough?
- Choose a fasting type - Which fasting model best matches your spiritual and behavioral goals?
- Dedicate time for worship, prayer, and reading Scripture.
- Exercise caution when breaking your fast. If you've chosen to refrain from food, end your fast gradually with nutritious options.

Fasting provides spiritual benefits that bring us closer to God. It is a powerful tool for spiritual growth. When done with the right heart, it deepens our faith, strengthens our spirit, and aligns us with God's purpose. It's not about earning favors but about drawing near to the One who sustains us. It plays a crucial role in renewing our minds. Just like fasting, our next habit is one of the missing jewels of the modern church.

Habit Eight: Confession - A Path to Forgiveness and Healing

Confession is an essential part of the Christian life. It involves acknowledging our sins before God and, when appropriate, before others. It is not merely an admission of wrongdoing but a step toward repentance, healing, and restoration. Confession deepens our relationship with God, strengthens our integrity, and encourages spiritual growth. It starts with our conversation with God.

If we confess our sins, he is faithful and just to forgive us our sins and to cleanse us from all unrighteousness. (1 John 1:9)

The Greek word translated as "confess" expresses our ability and willingness to recognize our behavior as God does. Our confession cannot justify us; instead, it must acknowledge sin as God perceives it. This concern addresses the heart and guidance of the Holy Spirit. This verse highlights key truths about confession: God is faithful and always responds to a sincere confession with forgiveness because He is just; forgiveness is available through Christ's sacrifice on the cross; and it is God's cleansing power that brings purification and restoration to our lives through confession.

Confession plays a vital role in our spiritual lives. Since sin separates us from God, confession restores our fellowship with Him. It brings spiritual cleansing as God purifies our hearts and renews our minds and spirits (Psalm 51:10). Recognizing our sin helps us see our need for God's grace as He encourages humility in our lives (James 4:10). Often, confessing our sins to God is the easy part; admitting our sins to others is much more difficult.

Confession also involves others in our lives. Sharing our confessions promotes accountability and emotional healing.

Therefore, confess your sins to one another and pray for one another, that you may be healed. The prayer of a righteous person has great power as it is working. (James 5:16)

While confessing to God brings forgiveness, confessing to others promotes healing and accountability. Sharing our struggles helps weaken the power of sin in our lives as our secrets are revealed. Sin flourishes in secrecy, but confession exposes it to the light (Ephesians 5:11). Confiding in others and confessing encourage prayer and strengthen us (Ecclesiastes 4:9-10). When confession becomes a habit, having accountability partners helps us stay on the right path (Proverbs 27:17).

At times, confession arises from a confrontation by someone who loves us. We are reminded of this through the story of David. We read the tragic account of David's failure in 2 Samuel 11-12. David is at home and notices a beautiful woman bathing on the house's rooftop next door. He asks his servants, "Who is this woman?" They inform him that it is Bathsheba, Uriah's wife. I must pause in this story because there is an important point related to maintaining relationships in which people feel free to confront us.

I am amazed that David had to ask! Had David lost touch with one of his closest friends? Scripture reminds us that David spent nearly 20 years hiding in caves from King Saul, waiting for Israel to fully accept him as king. David was surrounded by his "thirty mighty men" (2 Samuel 23), who fought alongside him during this time. They were his closest friends. Uriah was among those friends, and David seemingly lost track of him, not realizing that the man and woman next door were Uriah and Bathsheba. It is costly when we drift from our accountability relationships. The story continues.

David commands his servants to bring her to him. He sleeps with her, and she becomes pregnant. Through deception and trickery, he tries to persuade Uriah to return from the war and spend a few nights with his wife. Instead, Uriah, always obedient and a loyal friend, sleeps outside David's house. In a final act of desperation, David sends a note to Joab with Uriah, instructing that Uriah be placed at the front lines of battle without support. Uriah is killed, and David believes his "problem is hidden and solved." However, Nathan, the prophet of God, knows the entire story and confronts David, who confesses and mourns. Later, David writes Psalm 51.

Have mercy on me, O God, according to your unfailing love; according to your great compassion blot out my transgressions. Wash away all my iniquity and cleanse me from my sin. For I know my transgressions, and my sin is always before me. Against you, you only, have I sinned and done what is evil in your sight. (Psalm 51:1-4)

David's confession teaches us to keep our friends close and approach God with a humble, repentant heart. It reminds us how hard it can be to admit and confess our faults to others.

Many people find it difficult to confess due to fear, pride, or shame. John Powell once said that we struggle because we are afraid others might think less of us. Confession is a tool God uses to foster humility and authenticity in our lives. It provides incredible spiritual and emotional benefits.

- Peace with God - A clear conscience fosters inner peace (Philippians 4:6-7).
- Stronger relationships - Honesty enhances the bonds of friendship between individuals.
- Spiritual Growth - Confession strengthens our faith and holiness.
- Greater Joy and Freedom - Living in truth brings joy and freedom (John 8:32).
- Renewing the mind - Confession is an essential practice that enhances our understanding of His will while transforming the mind.

Confession is a valuable gift from God that offers forgiveness, healing, and renewed strength. When we humbly admit our sins —both to God and, when needed, to others—we experience His grace and renewal. By confessing a regular part of our spiritual walk, we draw nearer to God and live in the freedom of His forgiveness.

Habit Nine: Sabbath and Rest - Embracing God's Rhythm of Renewal

Sabbath and rest are essential for a balanced and spiritually healthy life. In a world that emphasizes constant productivity, God calls His people to set aside time for rest and focus on Him.

The Sabbath is more than just stopping work; it is about renewal, worship, and trusting in God's provision.

The challenge for most of us is that we have learned to worship the curse. A rereading of Genesis reminds us of this tragic story. God created man and woman and placed them in a garden where they were to work, pruning and harvesting. In the garden's center stood two trees – the Tree of the Knowledge of Good and Evil and the Tree of Life. They were encouraged to eat from the Tree of Life and to avoid the other tree. At some point in the story, Eve encounters a serpent. It is not until the Book of Revelation that the serpent is finally identified as Satan (Revelation 12:9). Harold Myra captures the moment Eve eats the fruit in the novel The Choice (pgs 47-48).

> The flesh of the fruit looked more succulent than any she had seen, a light peach color with a slight purple toward the center. As she tore away a piece, the color darkened into a deeper purple at the pit. She pushed the piece into her mouth. The taste was unique, delicious. She bit into it again, flashes of exotic ecstasy flowing through her, but a strange sense of alarm also tearing at her emotions. Juice ran down her chin; she wiped it off with her fingers as well as she could and turned to look at the serpent. She wanted to say something about fruit with her ally in this deed. . .
>
> Risha wanted more of the fruit. She desired to repeat the initial ecstasy of that first taste. She wanted to lose herself forever in that shocking pleasure that would smother the new voices within her.
>
> She bit into another and quickly ate it, skin and all. But it was not as satisfying as that first taste. She ate another, and then another. As she rapidly chewed and swallowed, a new sensation of continuing hunger and thirst demanded ever more fruit. Always before she had been pleasantly satisfied in eating.
>
> Risha looked again at the serpent, at his detached expression, and this time she understood fully that he had

deceived her. Her mouth went dry. She felt rage and horror at the enormity of her deed. She strode over to the serpent, shaking, her eyes tight and burning. 'You *lied!*' she spat at him. 'You are the evil. All that you said were lies!'

Satan misled Eve about the "true nature" of the fruit, and she chose to take a bite. Her life changed forever at that moment. She must have thought, "I need to get Adam to eat the fruit."

She hands Adam the fruit, and he now faces a crucial choice. If he eats it in disobedience, he will lose God but keep Eve. If he remains obedient and refuses to eat it, he will lose Eve but maintain his fellowship with God. Paul reminds us in Romans 5:12 that sin entered humanity through Adam, not Eve. She was deceived, but he made a decision that affected us all. Immediately, the couple became aware of their nakedness and hid from the Lord.

They finally admit to eating the fruit. The Lord delivers several curses. The Devil will face judgment. Eve's relationship with Adam will change, and Adam will now have to work much harder to earn a living. To Adam, He said,

Because you listened to your wife and ate from the tree about which I commanded you, 'You must not eat of it,' Cursed is the ground because of you; through painful toil you will eat of it all the days of your life. It will produce thorns and thistles for you, and you will eat the plants of the field. By the sweat of your brow you will eat your food until you return to the ground, since from it you were taken; for dust you are and to dust you will return. (Genesis 3:17-19)

Over the years, we have developed a work philosophy that recognizes the curse influencing how we view work.

Instead of seeing "overwork" as a curse, we appreciate people who put in a lot of effort. We call this the Protestant Work Ethic. I grew up thinking that unless I was constantly being productive, I was lazy and not measuring up. I remember working in health care, cutting short vacations to spend time with my family because "I was needed at work." I believed I had only two choices: bring my briefcase on vacation to work whenever I could or shorten my vacation to be productive at the hospital. It took me years to get rid of the guilt I felt when I wasn't working. I had to learn the value of taking a Sabbath and set aside regular time to relax.

The Sabbath is a commandment from God that reflects His plan for human well-being. Exodus 20:8 states: "Remember the Sabbath day, to keep it holy." This commandment highlights three main aspects:

- Remembering - Sabbath is a time to reflect on and honor God's work in creation and redemption.
- Holiness - The day is designated as sacred and separate from the rest of the week.
- Resting - A pause from regular work to rejuvenate the body and spirit.

The Sabbath is a divine gift designed to imitate God's rest, renew our strength, and deepen our worship. It allows us to focus on God without distractions (Psalm 46:10) and to trust in His provision. Taking a break from work shows faith that God will provide (Exodus 16:23-30), just as Jesus demonstrated the importance of the Sabbath.

Jesus emphasized the importance of the Sabbath while addressing legalistic views about it. He made it clear that the Sabbath is a gift for people, not a burden.

The Sabbath was made for man, not man for the Sabbath. (Mark 2:27)

He taught that the Sabbath is not about strict rules but about experiencing rest, healing, and renewal in God's presence. He performed acts of mercy and healing on the Sabbath, showing that true rest includes spiritual renewal. He was raised in an environment that formally observed the Sabbath. While traditional Sabbath observance happens on Saturday, many Christians see Sunday as a day for worship and rest in celebration of Christ's resurrection. Still, the idea of Sabbath rest goes beyond just one day—it includes a way of life focused on trusting God and seeking spiritual renewal. Here are some practical ways to bring Sabbath and rest into your daily routine. Pick a day for worship and reflection. Go to church and participate in communal worship (Hebrews 10:25). Set aside extra time for prayer and Scripture meditation (Psalm 119:15). Give thanks for God's blessings (Colossians 3:16-17). Disconnect from work and stress by taking breaks from emails, work duties, and excessive screen time. Engage in relaxing activities like nature walks, journaling, or peaceful reading. Prioritize your relationships with family and friends. Engage in acts of mercy and joy. Serve others in a way that brings happiness instead of stress (Luke 6:9). Encourage and fellowship with one another (Romans 12:10-11). Take time for creative and restorative hobbies. Trust God with your productivity. Sabbath rest is an act of faith that shows our success depends on God, not endless work (Matthew 6:25-34). It highlights that true rest comes from abiding in Christ (John 15:4-5).

We must remember that taking time to observe the Sabbath is essential. Many struggle to rest because of busy schedules, feelings of guilt, or cultural pressure. Prioritizing Sabbath rest is a crucial part of spiritual health. Remember that rest is a command, not just a suggestion—God designed it for your well-being. If you can't take a full day off, set aside intentional time for spiritual renewal; this remains important.

We experience renewed strength and emotional and physical refreshment when we observe Sabbath rest. Developing this habit promotes greater peace as we trust in God rather than depending solely on our efforts. As this practice becomes established, we deepen our relationship with God and focus more on His presence. We nurture a heart centered on worship instead of worry. The Sabbath represents a divine rhythm of rest, worship, and renewal. By dedicating time to rest and focus on God, we encounter His peace and provision in new ways. Embracing Sabbath rest helps us align our lives with God's design and find true refreshment for our souls.

Habit Ten: Giving - A Heart of Generosity and Worship

Giving is a vital part of the Christian life. It includes not only finances but also the giving of our time, talents, and resources as acts of worship and trust in God. In American culture, it often begins with financial giving. Biblical giving reflects gratitude, faith, and a desire to bless others. It is a tangible way to show love for God and others. Financial giving demonstrates trust in God as the provider for His children.

A week after getting married, I realized that I now needed to manage the finances in my new home. I was twenty, and for some reason, I hadn't thought much about finances, budgeting, or giving—after all, I was in love. I asked my dad how he managed his finances, checkbook, budget, and spending. I remember he pulled out his checkbook and showed me that the first check he wrote each month was for the Lord. He tithed ten percent of his pay each month as his baseline giving.

"The first check you should write each month is the one to the Lord," he said. "If you don't, you might find nothing left after you finish paying the bills."

LouAnna and I have followed his advice for over sixty years. Throughout our life together, God has consistently met our needs and fulfilled many of our desires. Generosity begins with a heart of obedience. Giving is a command. Both obedience and generosity are works of the Holy Spirit.

The Bible teaches that generosity reflects God's giving.

Each of you should give what you have decided in your heart to give, not reluctantly or under compulsion, for God loves a cheerful giver. (2 Corinthians 9:7)

This verse highlights three key principles of giving:

- It's a personal choice. Giving should be motivated by kindness, not by pressure.
- It should be done willingly; God prefers joyful giving

over hesitant or regretful donations.

- God is pleased; a cheerful giver displays God's generous nature. Jesus highlighted that generosity reflects God's kingdom.

Give, and it will be given to you. A good measure, pressed down, shaken together and running over, will be poured into your lap. For with the measure you use, it will be measured to you. (Luke 6:38)

Giving is met with God's abundant blessings, not only in material wealth but also in spiritual and relational rewards. It is not just a duty; it is a spiritual discipline that deepens our faith. Giving recognizes that everything we have comes from Him as our provider (Deuteronomy 8:18). Sacrificial giving reminds us that God is our source (Malachi 3:10). When we give, it reinforces our trust in God's provision. Financial gifts support ministries, missions, and those in need (Philippians 4:15-17). Just as God brought Israel out of Egypt, He instructed them to fully support the priests and their work. God has designated that His people fund His work. Giving shifts our focus from possessions to God's kingdom (Matthew 6:19-21). Since many Americans live as if their God is money, we must start giving with our finances. Today's currency includes not only money but also our time. Giving is not limited to money; it encompasses time, talents, and other resources. In subtle ways, our giving reveals our trust in God's provision.

We live in Satan's domain. One of his strongest temptations involves giving. He plants seeds of doubt and uncertainty as he leads us to fill our schedules with activities that lack eternal value. We become too busy to show generosity with our time. He encourages us to believe that we are the providers of our income. It's our money! Satan successfully shifts our focus from trusting God for everything to relying on our own wisdom and decision-making skills to handle our time and money. Giving generously requires a mindset change from Satan's way to God's. Scripture reminds us that all we have belongs to God. The question is not how much of my money I should give, but how much of God's money I should keep. We are stewards of God's resources.

When we give, we experience a deeper faith as we trust God to provide for us. Givers enjoy the blessing of helping others. Jesus reminded his followers that we reap eternal rewards by "storing treasures in heaven" (Matthew 6:20). Our giving meets the needs of the Body of Christ and helps the church impact the surrounding community. Giving is an act of worship, trust, and love. Whether through finances, time, or talents, generosity reflects God's character and advances His kingdom. As we give cheerfully and sacrificially, we grow spiritually and bless others. Unknowingly, our giving (or lack of it) influences the renewal of our minds.

Habit Eleven: Silence and Solitude - Drawing Near to God

Every now and then go away, have a little relaxation,
for when you come back to your work your judgment will be surer.
Go some distance away because
then the work appears smaller
and more of it can be taken in at a glance
and a lack of harmony and proportion
is more readily seen.
(Leonardo da Vinci)

Leonardo da Vinci's wisdom is often overlooked in a culture that prizes hard work. Silence and solitude are vital spiritual practices that allow us to withdraw from distractions and intentionally connect with God. In a world full of noise and activity, these practices help us listen to God, contemplate His truth, and depend more on Him. Yet, reaching this goal remains difficult.

Jesus Himself exemplified silence and solitude, showing their importance for spiritual renewal.

Very early in the morning, while it was still dark, Jesus got up, left the house and went off to a solitary place, where he prayed.

(Mark 1:35)

Jesus took time to be alone with the Father. He sought a quiet spot to focus on prayer, where he could escape distractions. Time alone with God strengthened him for his ministry. Jesus followed Old Testament examples and sought silence and solitude with God. Figures like Moses, Elijah, and David experienced moments when being alone with God in silence and solitude was essential.

These habits are essential because they help us hear God's voice. In stillness, we become more aware of His guidance. (Psalm 46:10) As we spend time with the Lord, our prayer life deepens, and solitude offers us uninterrupted communion with God. Being alone with the Lord often provides spiritual clarity as the external noise lessens, allowing us to reflect on His truth. It is amazing how even a brief time alone with God refreshes our souls as He renews our strength. Solitude reminds us that our strength comes from Him, not from our own efforts (John 15:5). Building a habit of silence and solitude requires intentional effort.

Here are practical ways to incorporate these disciplines into daily life:

Choose a specific time and place. Find a peaceful spot where you won't be disturbed. Pick the best time — early morning, evening, or during breaks.

Start with prayer and Scripture. Ask God to speak to you as you calm your heart. Reflect on a passage from Scripture (Psalm 1:2).

Practice listening to God. Instead of always talking in prayer, take time to simply listen. Pay attention to how the Holy Spirit may be guiding you.

Use a journal to reflect during your meditation. Write down your thoughts, prayers, or insights from your time alone. Observe how God is working in your life.

Embrace a stillness free of distractions. Turn off electronics and step back from life's busyness. Learn to find comfort in silence, resisting the urge to fill it with noise.

At the same time, you must overcome the challenges of silence and solitude. Many struggle with this habit due to busyness, restlessness, or distractions. If you are too busy, start with 5 to 10 minutes and gradually increase your time. If you are distracted, write down your intrusive thoughts in your journal to help you refocus. Those who feel restless find relief by asking God for help to be still and trust Him (Psalm 37:7). Are you feeling distant from God? Silence and solitude can help you reconnect with His presence. This is a crucial part of renewing our minds. By putting in the effort to develop this habit, we will unlock many blessings that go beyond just renewing the mind.

When we intentionally set aside time to be alone with God, we experience greater peace. Our anxiety and stress decrease as we rest in Him. We develop a deeper relationship with God by becoming more attuned to His voice and Word. Time alone with Him fosters spiritual renewal, strengthening our faith. Even our ministry and service become more effective. Just as Jesus withdrew for solitude before major events, we gain wisdom and strength for what lies ahead. Silence and solitude are not about isolation; they are about drawing closer to God. In quiet moments, we hear His voice more clearly, renew our strength, and grow in our dependence on Him. By making time to be still before the Lord, we deepen our relationship with Him and find the rest our souls need. During these times, as our minds are renewed, our vision of Him and His plan for our lives becomes clearer.

Habit Twelve: Stewardship - Faithfully Managing God's Gifts

Stewardship is the biblical principle of managing everything God has entrusted to us—our time, talents, finances, relationships, and even the environment. It recognizes that everything belongs to God, and we are simply caretakers called to use His gifts wisely and for His glory.

For over fifteen years, I dedicated two to three weeks each year to backpacking in Northern California and Oregon. I grew up without considering my role in preserving nature and the environment. Conservative Christians generally believed that all the attention "liberals" paid to the environment was a waste of time.

Backpacking compelled me, through silence and solitude, to reflect on my role as a Christian steward. The concept of stewardship begins in Genesis, where God places Adam in the Garden of Eden.

The Lord God took the man and put him in the Garden of Eden to work it and take care of it. (Genesis 2:15)

From the beginning, humanity has been entrusted with caring for and managing what God has given us. As I reflect on this passage, other key scriptures about stewardship come to mind. The earth is the Lord's, and everything in it, the world, and all who live in it (Psalm 24:1). Now it is required that those who have been given a trust must prove faithful (1 Corinthians 4:2). The Parable of the Talents teaches that we must wisely use what God entrusts to us (Matthew 25:14-30).

Stewardship covers all parts of life. As God's stewards, we oversee our time, talents, gifts, finances, and the environment. Time is a limited resource, and God calls us to use it wisely. We are called to make the most of every opportunity. This involves prioritizing God's kingdom as the most important aspect while striking a balance between work and rest. Make the best use of the time, because the days are evil (Ephesians 5:16). Seek first the kingdom of God and his righteousness, and all these things will be added to you (Matthew 6:33). God has given each person unique skills and spiritual gifts to serve Him and others. We must use our gifts for His glory (1 Peter 4:10). Just as the servants in the Parable of the Talents invested wisely, we should develop our abilities for God's purposes (Matthew 25:14-30). Serving others with our gifts is part of our stewardship (Romans 12:6-8). Managing money wisely shows our trust in

God's provision and involves responsible stewardship of our finances. We need to acknowledge that God owns everything. Stewardship involves giving generously (Proverbs 3:9) and managing our resources wisely, so we can provide for ourselves and bless others (Proverbs 22:7).

God has entrusted humanity with the responsibility of caring for the earth, calling us to be good stewards of creation. This means taking care of nature by avoiding waste and encouraging sustainability. Making efforts to protect the environment ensures that future generations can also enjoy God's creation. Stewardship is a way of life that acknowledges God as the owner of everything. By responsibly managing our time, talents, finances, and the environment, we honor Him and contribute to His kingdom. When we embrace stewardship, we grow spiritually, bless others, and enjoy the joy of living in harmony with God's will.

Summary

Habit one: Spending quality time in the Bible and meditation.
   Frequency: Ranges from daily to no less than three times weekly.

Habit Two: Spend regular and consistent time in prayer.
   Frequency: Daily

Habit Three: Fellowship in the Church - Strengthening the Body of Christ
   Frequency: Ranges from weekly to several times a week. This includes small group activities and special church events.

Habit Four: Service - Living Out Christ's Love
   Frequency: Ranges from weekly to several times a week. Can include service at church as well as community or neighborly service.

Habit Five: Evangelism - Sharing the Good News of Jesus Christ
   Frequency: At every feasible opportunity.

Habit Six: Worshiping the God We Love

Frequency: Ranges from daily to several times a week. This is done when we give, attend church, study the Word, pray, fast, practice solitude, practice sabbath, and other times of reflection.

Habit Seven: Fasting - Drawing Near to God
Frequency: Ranges from daily (intermittent fasting) to once or twice a year during special times of prayer and remembrance.

Habit Eight: Confession - A Path to Forgiveness and Healing
Frequency: Ranges from daily (during our prayer) to weekly or occasionally as we meet with other accountability opportunities.

Habit Nine: Sabbath and Rest - Embracing God's Rhythm of Renewal
Frequency: Ranges from weekly to every several months.

Habit Ten: Giving - A Heart of Generosity and Worship
Frequency: Ranges from weekly to monthly.

Habit Eleven: Silence and Solitude - Drawing Near to God
Frequency: Ranges from weekly to every several months.

Habit Twelve: Stewardship - Faithfully Managing God's Gifts
Frequency: Daily

As we finish this chapter, a summary is needed. Our desire to please God starts with understanding His will. It all begins with accepting the gospel of Jesus Christ, the only way to have a relationship with God. Joining God's family puts us on the path He planned for us. As we begin our journey with the Lord, we must dedicate ourselves fully to Him, resisting the urge to adopt the mindset of the surrounding culture. Our complete transformation requires ongoing renewal of our minds—a process achieved by practicing the twelve habits of the Christian life. As these habits become part of our lives, we notice small changes. Our next chapter will introduce you to the transformations you can expect.

Reflect & Respond

As you finish this chapter, take a few quiet moments to reflect on what God might be speaking to your heart. These questions help you remember key truths, deepen your understanding, challenge your assumptions, and motivate you to action. Whether you're working through them alone or with a group, invite the Holy Spirit to guide your thoughts, encourage honest conversations, and reveal the next step in your walk with Christ. Let this be not just a review but a response of faith, obedience, and transformation.

1. What is the biblical basis for developing spiritual habits according to 1 Timothy 4:7-8, and why are these habits essential to the Christian life?

2. How do spiritual habits differ from basic religious rituals or routines, and why is their importance for lasting transformation highlighted in this chapter?

3. How do the essential spiritual habits contribute to a life that honors God?"

4. How does regularly reading Scripture contribute to mind renewal and spiritual transformation?

5. What are at least three biblical benefits of regularly fellowshipping with other believers, and why is the idea that "I can love Jesus but not the Church" inconsistent with Scripture?

6. What distinguishes casual social interaction from biblical fellowship, and how can fellowship foster spiritual growth?

7. How can ordinary moments transform into acts of worship, and in what ways does consistent obedience in small things cultivate a life that pleases God?

8. How can regular fasting and confession refresh your mind and fully align your life with God's will?

9. How does your current allocation of time, talents, and finances reflect your understanding of biblical stewardship, and how could it be developed further?

10. Which spiritual habit do you currently find most challenging (e.g., prayer, fellowship, service), and what specific step can you take this week to strengthen it? How might silence, solitude, or stewardship aid you in this growth?

CHAPTER EIGHT

WHAT DOES PLEASING
THE LORD LOOK LIKE?

The smile of God is the deepest fuel of the soul.
When you know He is pleased, nothing else matters.
John Piper (paraphrased)

For this reason, since the day we heard about you, we have not stopped praying for you and asking God to fill you with the knowledge of his will through all spiritual wisdom and understanding. And we pray this in order that you may live a life worthy of the Lord and may please him in every way: bearing fruit in every good work, growing in the knowledge of God, being strengthened with all power according to his glorious might so that you may have great endurance and patience, and joyfully giving thanks to the Father, who has qualified you to share in the inheritance of the saints in the kingdom of light. For he has rescued us from the dominion of darkness and brought us into the kingdom of the Son he loves, in whom we have redemption, the forgiveness of sins. (Colossians 1:3-14)

Revisiting Paul's prayer in his letter to the Colossians helps us understand what it means to please the Lord. Paul uses four participles to describe a life that is pleasing to the Lord: bearing fruit, growing in knowledge, being strengthened, and giving thanks.

Bearing fruit in every good work

Paul's letter to the Ephesians reveals the spiritual truth that God has created a pathway for each of us, involving good works (Ephesians 2:10). The Greek word "good" is best understood as "beneficial." Every day, we face opportunities to make a difference in someone's life. A believer who follows God's will recognizes these chances to serve and takes action to create a positive impact. Jesus reminded his disciples of the key to being fruitful the night before his death.

No branch can bear fruit by itself; it must remain in the vine. Neither can you bear fruit unless you remain in me. (John 15:4)

This is to my Father's glory, that you bear much fruit, showing yourselves to be my disciples. (John 15:8)

In the natural world, fruit shows that a tree is healthy and fulfilling its purpose. In spiritual life, fruit symbolizes our connection to Christ and alignment with the Holy Spirit. Jesus made it clear that bearing fruit is not optional, but a key sign of a true disciple.

The believer who develops the habit of renewing their mind lives according to God's will—His perfect, mature, acceptable, and good will (Romans 12:2). As they maintain these habits, their life begins to grow and mature. Because they are filled with God's will, they stay connected to Jesus as He produces fruit in their lives.

What is this "fruit"?

Part of the answer is found in Galatians 5:22-23. The fruit of the Spirit includes love, joy, peace, patience, kindness, goodness, faithfulness, gentleness, and self-control. These qualities are not achieved by simply trying harder but by drawing closer to Jesus. They develop in us as we abide in the Vine. This fruit also includes the good works that come from our faith—acts of service, generosity, encouragement, and a life that reflects the grace we've received (Colossians 1:10). Furthermore, fruit isn't just personal; it's relational and missional. It's about helping others find and follow Jesus. Paul referred to his converts in Rome as "fruit" (Romans 1:13), reminding us that our lives are meant to multiply life in others. Scripture reminds us there is no better time than now to start being fruitful.

> *Be very careful, then, how you live —not as unwise but as wise, making the most of every opportunity, because the days are evil. Therefore do not be foolish, but understand what the Lord's will is. (Ephesians 5:15-17)*

In Shakespeare's *Julius Caesar* (*Act 4, Scene 3*), Brutus declares:

> "There is a tide in the affairs of men,
> Which, taken at the flood, leads on to fortune;
> Omitted, all the voyage of their life
> Is bound in shallows and in miseries.
> On such a full sea are we now afloat,
> And we must take the current when it serves,
> Or lose our ventures."

Shakespeare uses the formal definition of the Latin word "opportunus" as a powerful metaphor that highlights the importance of seizing opportunities. When the tide is high, ships can sail far; miss the moment, and the chance is gone. The original word was a nautical term reflecting the ebb and flow of the tide. "The word is a combination of the prefix ob, meaning 'to,' and portus, a word for a port or harbor. It originally alluded to choosing any port in a storm for safety" (Merriam-Webster). For sailing vessels, picking the right tide determined whether they could leave port. Brutus asserts that, just as sailors must ride the tide at its peak to reach their destination successfully, individuals must seize opportunities at the right moment in life. If they hesitate, they risk failure and regret.

He talks about fleeting opportunities in life—moments when taking decisive action can lead to success, but missing these chances can result in regret and stagnation. The metaphor is vivid: a ship must set sail when the tide is high or it will be stranded in the shallows.

Centuries before Shakespeare, the Apostle Paul conveyed a deeper and timeless truth in his letter to the Ephesians. He cautioned believers to live with wisdom and purpose, urging them to make the most of their time—that is, to prioritize every moment for God's plan. Why? Because "the days are evil." Cultural currents often incline us toward compromise, distraction, or indifference. Yet God's people are called to respond differently—with urgency and wisdom.

Paul does not seek action solely for success but to align with God's will. Wisdom is not just a good strategy; it is a Spirit-led way of living. God has preordained opportunities for each of us (Ephesians 2:10), and our challenge is not to create them but to recognize and respond to them.

If we apply this principle to our lives, we will:

- Sense the moment by asking God to reveal where He is opening doors today. Waiting for perfect conditions is a waste of time (Ecclesiastes 11:4).
- Act with wisdom instead of impulsiveness. Urgency can often cause quick, instinctive reactions. Seek God's Word and counsel before taking action.
- Be alert and watchful instead of distracted. Social noise, busyness, and fear can blind you to the spiritual opportunities that surround you. Silence your soul and tune into God's leading.

Today's believer has a remarkable advantage over those who lived before Jesus: we have the Holy Spirit. In the Old Testament, the Holy Spirit would come and go, and it was rare for someone to experience His presence throughout their entire life. On the day of Pentecost, the church was born, marked by the continuous presence of the Holy Spirit in every believer. The Holy Spirit represents God's presence and activity today; He convicts people of their sins, draws them to repentance, and helps them understand their need for salvation. The Holy

Spirit works in and through believers, guiding and empowering them for service, worship, and righteous living. Once He begins His work, He sustains the continuation and practical effects of maintaining spiritual habits.

Jesus referred to the Holy Spirit as a "Comforter" or "Advocate" (John 14:16), who would lead believers into all truth. Many Christians experience the Holy Spirit as a source of wisdom, helping them understand Scripture and discern God's will. In Acts 1:8, Jesus promised His disciples that they would receive power when the Holy Spirit came upon them. This empowerment enables Christians to fulfill God's mission, often manifesting in spiritual gifts and bold testimonies. As our new habits persist, we notice changes resulting from the Holy Spirit's presence and work.

The indwelling Spirit transforms our hearts and minds to reflect Christ's character. This process, known as sanctification, enables believers to grow in holiness and spiritual maturity. The Spirit also promotes unity among believers, breaks down barriers, and fosters a deep sense of fellowship and community within the Church. As Paul writes to the Church of Ephesus, he reminds them (Ephesians 5:10) that expressing God's will in one's life is pleasing to the Lord. His solution is to be filled with the Holy Spirit. The term "filled" connotes control, similar to being influenced by alcohol. He does not teach that living a Spirit-filled life means being numb or out of sync with our environment, but rather that Spirit-filled people experience a reduction in their own will and an increase in God's control and influence in how they think and live.

> *Do not get drunk on wine, which leads to debauchery. Instead, be filled with the Spirit. Speak to one another with psalms, hymns and spiritual songs. Sing and make music in your heart to the Lord, always giving thanks to God the Father for everything, in the name of our Lord Jesus Christ. Submit to one another out of reverence for Christ. (Ephesians 5:18-21)*

I've quoted the key verse from the NIV Bible. When the

NIV translators encountered Paul's long sentences in Greek, they often split them into several shorter ones. Typically, these changes create a translation that conveys the overall meaning of the writer but may overlook the nuances of the original text. Ephesians 5:18-21 serves as a classic example. In the original text, verses 18 through 21 form a single sentence, with the main verb being to be filled. Strangely, this verb is a passive imperative. Most commands are active, such as get the keys, go to the store, and come home. However, "Let me teach you" is a passive imperative. For someone to obey this command, they must stop resisting being taught and willingly become attentive to what is being taught. Paul implicitly suggests letting the Spirit take control of your life.

The rest of the sentence illustrates the characteristics of Spirit-filled individuals. The words "speak," "sing," "make music," "give thanks," and "submit" are participles that show how a Spirit-filled person behaves. When the Spirit takes control, we communicate differently, carry a song in our hearts, and create inner music while giving thanks and submitting to others. The Spirit produces Christlikeness within us. This behavior contradicts our natural tendency to revert to old ways of living and is only possible through the Holy Spirit. As we keep up our spiritual habits, our minds are renewed daily, allowing the Holy Spirit to have a greater influence in our lives as we live out God's will. A Spirit-controlled life spills over into our relationships, both at home and at work. It disarms those around us, encouraging them to seek answers to the behaviors they see in us. This new way of living was so attractive in the early church that God used it to draw thousands to the gospel and the community. We become fruitful. It is God's people acting and reflecting the Son. The enemy hates it.

Finally, be strong in the Lord and in his mighty power. Put on the full armor of God so that you can take your stand against the devil's schemes. For our struggle is not against flesh and blood, but against the rulers, against the authorities, against the powers of this dark world and against the spiritual forces of evil in the heavenly realms. (Ephesians 6:10-12)

Paul writes, "Finally," as he summarizes this section, which begins with describing the filling of the Spirit. Some people may react negatively when we show the fruit of the Spirit (Galatians 5:22-26). When others push us, we might mistakenly think they are the enemy. Paul quickly reminds us that they are not the problem; the real culprit is Satan. The next time someone tries to tell you what to do and you hear a voice in your head saying, "Who are you to tell me what to do?" that voice may be Satan or one of his angels. Spirit-filled individuals are servant leaders who understand where the real battle lines are and learn to surrender control to the Spirit.

As you read this, you might wonder, "How can I be filled with the Spirit?" The role of the Holy Spirit in a believer's life can be summarized in two words: ownership and maturity. First, the Holy Spirit acts as a down payment that guarantees our future (2 Corinthians 5:5). This is visible to the spiritual realm and signifies ownership. Maturity describes the process and result of the Spirit's inner work to shape us into the image of the Son (Romans 8:28-29). Most of God's will involves transforming us into Christ-like individuals. The convicting work of the Holy Spirit not only convinces non-believers of sin; it also prompts believers to change and grow into Christlikeness. God uses every resource available to encourage us to fully become like Him. The areas of growth can be grouped into five main categories: the church (Ephesians 4:11-16), our daily circumstances (James 1:1-8), our encounters with God's Word (2 Timothy 3:16-17), the people in our lives (Philippians 2:1-5), and God's direct engagement with our daily lives (Hebrews 12:1-12). In each area, the Holy Spirit prompts us to reflect on what we are hearing or experiencing. His goal is to help us take the next step.

The circumstances surrounding my encounter with the friend who accused me of hypocrisy show how the Holy Spirit seeks to fill us and take control. When I was confronted, I felt troubled. The Holy Spirit's work can often be uncomfortable and unsettling. I recognized that what my friend was saying was true, but I hoped his observations might be exceptions. However, when I asked another person, she confirmed my worst fears. On the drive home, I remember crying and feeling awful. The Holy Spirit was beginning His work in my life.

I woke up the next day feeling guilty. As the day progressed, I started to rationalize my behavior. While convincing myself that I was a loving person who had been misunderstood, the Holy Spirit was grieving (Ephesians 4:30). Looking back, I now realize that my indecision about changing caused grief to God; however, during those uncertain days, I kept justifying my unloving actions. No matter how hard I tried, I couldn't ignore the truth that I needed to stop my hypocrisy and be authentic. If I continued to resist the prompting of the Holy Spirit, I risked quenching the Spirit (1 Thessalonians 5:19). When we "put out the Spirit's fire" (NIV), He stops convicting us. He leaves us to wander in rebellion and immaturity. Eventually, He will use another event, person, passage, or memory to persuade us again. He won't give up. He immediately prompts us to change when we read the Bible or experience something. He empowers us to succeed and grow into Christlikeness when we acknowledge His prompting and let Him guide us. Some of us have spent a lifetime suppressing the Holy Spirit's work. As we grow, we begin to walk in the Spirit regularly and show the fruit of the Spirit in our lives—the character of Jesus.

> But the fruit of the Spirit is love, joy, peace, patience, kindness, goodness, faithfulness, gentleness and self-control. Against such things there is no law. Those who belong to Christ Jesus have crucified the sinful nature with its passions and desires. Since we live by the Spirit, let us keep in step with the Spirit. Let us not become conceited, provoking and envying each other. (Galatians 5:22-26)

One of the biggest myths we can accept is that God will shape us into Christ's likeness without our active participation in spiritual practices and the Holy Spirit's power. Our issue is that we often forget we are in a divine partnership. We need to remember that experiencing God's plan depends on our involvement. When we fully commit, resist living according to the pattern of this world, and embrace the transformation that comes from renewing our minds as we develop proper habits, God's will becomes clearer. Peter understood this as he wrote his last letter, describing the process of growth and maturity that begins as our new habits lead us closer to the Lord and His purpose for our lives (2 Peter 1:5-9). As these habits remain in our lives, we become more fruitful and grow nearer to God.

Growing in the knowledge of God.

A second characteristic of a life that pleases God is pursuing a closer relationship with Him. The Greek participle, 'growing,' is passive, suggesting that God actively reveals Himself to us more deeply when He is pleased with us. In his last letter, Peter encourages us by reminding us that grace and peace are abundantly available to the believer who knows Jesus and God the Father (2 Peter 1:2). The Greek word for knowledge is 'epiginosko,' which emphasizes an intimate understanding of another person. He knows our thoughts, and we are learning to trust Him fully. In his book *'Knowing God,'* J. I. Packer laments that most of us know about God, but very few truly know Him.

I grew up in a church that highly valued the Bible. We believed that knowing God was the same as knowing His Word, forming a large group of people who understood the Bible without truly knowing the author. God made us for relationships; He doesn't want us to study the Bible to learn about Him. He longs for a face-to-face relationship with His children, as shown in Moses's life.

The Lord would speak to Moses face to face, as a man speaks with his friend . . . Moses said to the Lord, "You have been telling me, 'Lead these people,' but you have not let me know whom you will send with me. You have said, 'I know you by name and you have found favor with me.' If you are pleased with me, teach me your ways so I may know you and continue to find favor with you. Remember that this nation is your people." The Lord replied, "My Presence will go with you, and I will give you rest." Then Moses said to him, "If your Presence does not go with us, do not send us up from here. How will anyone know that you are pleased with me and with your people unless you go with us? What else will distinguish me and your people from all the other people on the face of the earth?" And the Lord said to Moses, "I will do the very thing you have asked, because I am pleased with you and I know you by name. (Exodus 33:11-17)

This passage describes a confrontation between God and Israel. The narrative shows that after Moses told Israel to wait at the mountain's base, he went up to meet with God. He stayed longer than Israel expected. In their impatience and disobedience, they asked Aaron to make a golden calf, hoping to see the invisible God. Four hundred years had exposed them to the gods of Egypt. They may have left Egypt, but Egypt had not left them. They had already broken the first two commandments before Moses arrived. When Moses heard the noise of celebration, he came down the mountain and saw what they had done. He and God then talked, and God suggested a change of plans; He proposed to destroy Israel and start over with Moses. Moses begged for Israel's salvation, reminding God that they are His people. God agreed to continue with Israel, but Moses worried that God might abandon them in the wilderness. *Because He was pleased with Moses*, God promised to go before them as He led them to the Promised Land. Moses wanted to know God deeply, and God led him to a crevice in the mountain where he could experience God's passing by. The text continues.

And he passed in front of Moses, proclaiming, "The Lord, the Lord, the compassionate and gracious God, slow to anger, abounding in love and faithfulness, maintaining love to thousands, and forgiving wickedness, rebellion and sin. Yet he does not leave the guilty unpunished; he punishes the children and their children for the sin of the fathers to the third and fourth generation. (Exodus 34:6-7)

When God is pleased with us, He reveals who He is. God desires a relationship with us, but this only happens when we live according to His will. As He passes by Moses, the Lord reveals that He is compassionate and gracious, slow to anger, loving and faithful, and forgiving of "wickedness, rebellion, and sin." "Yet he does not leave the guilty unpunished." He justly punishes sin in every generation. He would not be God if He ignored sin. What is your view of God?

Studies suggest that many of us form our view of God based on humanity, culture, and those around us. In my experience, one of the most important influences in answering this question comes from how we perceive our fathers. Christian psychologists suggest that our relationship with our earthly father influences how we see our heavenly Father. If your father was angry and abusive, you might tend to describe God in a similar way. In a recent talk with several believers, most responded to this question by assuming God's initial response to disobedience was anger. They referenced the Old Testament and their experiences with friends and family. The best place to find answers is God Himself.

God tells Moses that He is slow to anger. The biblical narrative of the New Testament describes a God whose initial response to our disobedience is grief, not anger. The Old Testament clearly exemplifies God's patience in responding to disobedience. A small part of the story about Moses receiving the Law and the related ordinances shows God's concern for the land. In Leviticus 25:1-7, God commands Israel that once they enter the Promised Land, they must let the land rest every seventh year. This was an act of trust in God's provision and a spiritual discipline of stewardship over the land He had given them. Many years later, Israel was basically divided into two kingdoms: Northern Israel and Southern Israel. In 722 BC, Shalmaneser V, King of Assyria, conquered Northern Israel and took its people into captivity. In 605 BC, Daniel was taken by Nebuchadnezzar to Babylon, where he would spend his life. While in captivity, he read Jeremiah and learned the minimum length of time Israel would be in captivity.

> In the first year of Darius son of Xerxes (a Mede by descent), who was made ruler over the Babylonian kingdom— in the first year of his reign, I, Daniel, understood from the Scriptures, according to the word of the Lord given to Jeremiah the prophet, that the desolation of Jerusalem would last seventy years. (Daniel 9:1-2)

Ezra explains why the captivity would last for at least seventy years.

> He carried into exile to Babylon the remnant, who escaped from the sword, and they became servants to him and his sons until the kingdom of Persia came to power. The land enjoyed its sabbath rests; all the time of its desolation it rested, until the seventy years were completed in fulfillment of the word of the Lord spoken by Jeremiah. (2 Chronicles 36:20-21)

Once in the Promised Land, God gave Israel four hundred ninety years to observe the Land Sabbaths. As a nation, they ignored the command not to plant crops in the seventh year, missing seventy land Sabbaths. Partly, God allowed them to be taken into captivity so the land could enjoy all the Sabbaths it had missed. God is long-suffering and slow to anger.

The Lord is compassionate and gracious, slow to anger, and full of love and faithfulness. This truth forms the foundation of John's teaching that only those who love can truly know God.

> Dear friends, let us love one another, for love comes from God. Everyone who loves has been born of God and knows God. Whoever does not love does not know God, because God is love. (1 John 4:7–8)

When our lives please the Lord, we begin to understand and fully embrace the greatest commandment: to love the Lord our God with all our heart, soul, and mind, and to love our neighbor as ourselves. (Matthew 22:37-39).

When we live according to God's will, He starts to draw closer to us. James refers to this as a remedy for loving the world.

> *Submit yourselves, then, to God. Resist the devil, and he will flee from you. Come near to God and he will come near to you. Wash your hands, you sinners, and purify your hearts, you double-minded. Grieve, mourn and wail. Change your laughter to mourning and your joy to gloom. Humble yourselves before the Lord, and he will lift you up. (James 4:7-10)*

God's presence can be described in three ways. First, He is omnipresent (Psalm 139:7-10). All of Him is present everywhere in His creation at the same time. Second, He can be found in the throne room (Job 1:6 & Revelation 4). The third expression of His presence is personal; He is either near or far. This relational term captures the essence of our face-to-face relationship with Him. When His will guides us, we are pleasing to Him. As we seek to please Him, He draws nearer in ways that defy explanation. When we live according to worldly desires, He remains distant. However, He comes near when we please Him by renewing our minds. His nearness begins to reveal more about Himself through scripture and circumstances. This closeness provides a lens through which we view life.

As this process started, my desire to attend medical school faded. Instead, I developed a longing to serve others spiritually. Looking back now, I see that the life I once wanted wouldn't have fulfilled God's will, nor would it have been the best life for me. After years of ministering and allowing God to use me to introduce others to His plan in Scripture, I realize that His presence provided the life I always hoped for. I also understand that God strengthened me with the power to live out His purpose.

> *Grace and peace be yours in abundance through the knowledge of God and of Jesus our Lord. (2 Peter 1:2)*

We start this section with this verse in mind. As we grow

closer to God, we experience abundant grace and peace. Once again, Peter uses epiginosko to signify a type of knowledge that is personal and intimate. This originates from a relationship that pleases God and sets the stage for the work of the Holy Spirit.

Being strengthened with all power.

His divine power has given us everything we need for life and godliness through our knowledge of him who called us by his own glory and goodness. Through these he has given us his very great and precious promises, so that through them you may participate in the divine nature and escape the corruption in the world caused by evil desires. (2 Peter 1:3-4)

Peter initiates a transition to empowerment through the Holy Spirit by reminding us that this "knowledge of him" provides a "divine power" that guarantees victory in living the Christian life. Through His promises, we "participate in the divine nature and escape the corruption in the world caused by evil desires." We have everything we need to succeed in the Christian life. While cults add another book or teaching, Christianity requires only a relationship with the creator of the Universe. This encouragement comes with the reminder that pleasing God requires being filled with His will.

It pleases the Lord when we let Him be our source of strength. This reflects Paul's prayer for the believers in Colossae, where he explains what it means to please the Lord. He asks that they lead lives worthy of Christ, bearing fruit, growing in knowledge, and being strengthened for a specific purpose: endurance and patience.

When Paul writes, "Strengthened with All Power," he does not mean we should "try harder," but rather that we should "be strengthened" or continually empowered. This pleases God. He uses the Greek word dynamoumenoi, from which we get the English word dynamite. This strength is "according to His glorious might," referring to God's unlimited power, not our limited strength. It is the strength that raised Jesus from the dead (Ephesians 2:19). This is a recurring theme for Paul.

I pray that out of His glorious riches He may strengthen you with power through His Spirit in your inner being. (Ephesians 3:16)

The purpose of this strength is endurance and patience. Interestingly, Paul chose to connect God's strengthening to these two qualities. We might wonder why these two. Why not strengthen us in living life more fully or achieving our God-honored goals? Why not relate Paul's use of strengthening to his ministry? Paul will reveal this truth later in his letter to the Colossians, reminding us that his goal is to produce maturity in the believer's life with all the power God provides. (Colossians 1:28-29).

He emphasizes the importance of patience and endurance, as lacking these qualities often prevents us from pleasing God. Naturally, we tend to be impatient with both situations and people. The stoplight seems to stay red for too long, and the line at the store feels excessively slow. We struggle with waiting on the Lord. God is displeased when our impatience deprives us of the blessings, growth, and maturity that can only come through these qualities. Patience and endurance reflect our spiritual maturity and our relationship with the Holy Spirit. Paul begins with these qualities as the foundation for the discussion because they can either support or undermine our lives. Living out the will of God opens the door to the expression of His power in our lives. It manifests as patience.

The first demonstration of God's power is endurance (hypomone). This term refers to steadfastness in facing trials or remaining faithful under pressure. It is used in Scripture to describe "patience" with circumstances in our lives. It signifies perseverance and the ability to stand firm through suffering without giving up. It often relates to enduring difficult situations, hardships, pain, or persecution.

...suffering produces perseverance; perseverance, character; and

character, hope. (Romans 5:3-4)

Consider it pure joy, my brothers, whenever you face trials of many kinds, because you know that the testing of your faith develops perseverance. Perseverance must finish its work so that you may be mature and complete, not lacking anything. (James 1:2-4)

God strengthens us to endure long seasons of difficulty—illness, financial strain, ministry setbacks, or personal loss—without losing heart or giving up. In our book, *Spiritual Fitness: A Guide to Biblical Maturity,* Dr. Trammell and I identify *hypomone* as the precursor to maturity. Maturity develops only in part because of remaining in the struggle long enough to reap the benefits of growth.

It's easy to view our future through the lens of our circumstances and overlook the bigger picture. Yet, we are also promised hope and peace. Amidst life's storms, God has a plan for us. He intends to work "all things" together in our lives so that we reflect Jesus (Romans 8:28-29). We are people being transformed into His likeness daily (2 Corinthians 3:18), which can sometimes be painful. It's like being placed in a rock polisher.

Although we may not like it, "all things" include both the good and the bad. Years ago, our family got a rock polisher. We laugh about it now, but at the time, it drove us crazy! The polisher consisted of two hard rubber containers into which we dumped a handful of small stones, some grit, and water. It was placed on a platform that rotated nonstop. No matter where it was in the house, the hum of the polisher was always audible. Over the following months, we opened the container several times, washed the stones, and added smaller grit and more water. After a few months, we prepared for the final step. We mixed the stones with water and grit that had the consistency of talcum powder and listened to the hum for two more weeks.

None of us could believe the results. The stones were beautiful; all the rough edges had been smoothed down. You could see through them, and they felt smooth, looking nothing like the stones we started with. Rock polishing illustrates God's method of transforming a person into the likeness of His Son. The grit represents life's circumstances, while the other rocks symbolize the people in our lives. When we wish to be removed from the process, the polishing comes to a stop.

If we trust Him during this time of refining, when everything around us feels painful and hopeless, we will discover God's plan along with His peace, joy, and hope. His shalom continues to work on our behalf. Paul's prayer for the saints in Rome still speaks to us today: "May the God of hope fill you with all joy and peace as you trust in Him, so that you may overflow with hope by the power of the Holy Spirit." (Romans 15:13) God is pleased with us when we patiently endure the struggle.

The second word Paul uses is patience (makrothymia). In this context, patience refers to long-suffering with people, not situations. It is a fruit of the Spirit (Galatians 5:22) and involves showing mercy, kindness, and restraint even when wronged, annoyed, or provoked. This reflects God's own patience with sinners (cf. 2 Peter 3:9). God empowers us to be patient with difficult people—family, coworkers, fellow believers, and even enemies—reflecting His grace rather than reacting in anger. Why does it matter? It matters because 90% of God's will conform us into His Son's image. He uses circumstances and people to chip away at everything in us that doesn't resemble Jesus.

Endurance and patience are not natural; they are supernatural gifts from God's power in a believer's life. Together, these qualities reflect a Spirit-filled and mature life. They please the Lord and embody a way of living that we all desire. We must constantly seek the Spirit's strength through prayer and meditation on the Word, knowing that we cannot produce endurance or patience on our own. We should view hardships and relational tensions as opportunities for growth in endurance and patience, rather than setbacks. Wisdom guides us to "Consider it pure joy..." whenever we face trials... because we understand that testing our faith develops perseverance. Patience with circumstances shows our level of maturity, while patience with people indicates that the Holy Spirit is at work within us. We need to pause before reacting and choose grace over irritation. When feeling provoked by someone, take a moment to breathe a short prayer:

"Father, help me show the patience You have shown me."

Endurance and patience anchor us in God's bigger story. We live not just for the present but for eternity, trusting in God's plans, even when they are unseen.

You need to persevere so that when you have done the will of God, you will receive what He has promised. (Hebrews 10:36)

Colossians 1:11 teaches that God's strength empowers a life that genuinely pleases the Lord by demonstrating endurance through trials and patience with others. It may not be flashy or especially impressive to the world, but it is valuable to God— a faithful, Christlike heart that stays steady and gracious over time. At the same time, we experience joy. A life lived according to God's will not only pleases the Lord by bearing fruit, growing closer to Him, and being empowered by the Spirit, but also serves as a model of thankfulness in all circumstances.

Being filled with thankfulness.

Giving thanks to the Father, who has qualified you to share in the inheritance of the saints in the kingdom of light. For he has rescued us from the dominion of darkness and brought us into the kingdom of the Son he loves, in whom we have redemption, the forgiveness of sins. (Colossians 1:12-14)

Are you a "cup is half empty" or a "cup is half full" person? One trait of someone who pleases God is thankfulness. This might be difficult for you if you have a "cup is half empty" outlook. Unthankfulness often comes up when we face challenges, unmet expectations, or tough circumstances that make it hard to focus on gratitude. Here are a few common reasons:

Focusing on the negative.

Whether we're wired to focus on the negative or it's been a while since we were encouraged, it's easy to dwell on negative experiences, current struggles, or past hurts. This focus can cloud our view and make it harder to see the positive things around us.

Comparison with Others.

Comparing our lives to others, especially through social media, can cause feelings of dissatisfaction. Watching others' successes or blessings may make us feel inadequate, overshadowing the good things in our own lives. This comparison is an increasingly problematic issue, especially as social media often shows an exaggerated view of positive events happening around us. We end up questioning why our lives seem less exciting than those shown online.

Unmet Expectations.

When life doesn't go as planned or we don't get what we believe we deserve, it can cause disappointment. These unmet expectations can make us feel shortchanged, and gratitude may seem insincere. Unmet expectations can damage any relationship, including our relationship with the Lord. We are rarely thankful when a friend or God falls short of our expectations. When a prayer, for example, is answered, we think, "Well, it's about time."

Entitlement.

Sometimes, we feel we deserve a comfortable life, success, or good health. When these expectations aren't met, we may respond with resentment instead of gratitude.

Stress and Anxiety.

Daily pressures, anxiety about the future, and unresolved worries can overwhelm us, making it harder to recognize our blessings.

Lack of Perspective.
When we lose sight of the bigger picture, we may overlook small blessings or forget how far we've come. A lack of perspective often results in ingratitude.

Spiritual Disconnect.
For believers, a close relationship with God is the source of gratitude. When that connection weakens, it becomes easier to feel ungrateful or discontent. When we're ungrateful, it shows that we're missing the bigger picture – God has qualified us to share in an inheritance.

Thankfulness pleases God. We are encouraged to be thankful in all things and for all things. Here, Paul narrows our focus of thankfulness to what God has done for us. Our habit is to get lost in the small things of life: daily provisions, good friends, help in times of distress, and so on, and miss the significant accomplishments God provides for us. However, Paul draws our attention to the reality that we would not be thankful for anything if God had not qualified us to share in the inheritance of the saints.

Paul describes those who please God as believers whose lives are filled with gratitude toward the Father. This gratitude is not for what we have accomplished but for what God has done for us. Thanksgiving is the proper response when we recognize the greatness of God's grace. The Father qualifies us, not our works or religious performance. "Qualified" (Greek: hikanoō) means made sufficient, authorized, or made fit. The inheritance refers to eternal life with God, sharing His glory and blessings alongside all the saints.

In Him we have obtained an inheritance... (Ephesians 1:11)

Now if we are children, then we are heirs—heirs of God and co-heirs with Christ. (Romans 8:17)

The "Kingdom of light" represents God's realm of truth, righteousness, and glory. Light symbolizes life, purity, revelation, and God's presence. (John 8:12) We were rescued from the Dominion of Darkness, which signifies Satan's realm of sin, deception, and death. The Greek word *rhyomai* means we were delivered to God from danger and captivity. We were spiritually enslaved and powerless to free ourselves until God intervened. (Acts 26:18 and Ephesians 2:1-2). However, we were not merely rescued.

We were "brought into the Kingdom of the Son He loves." We weren't just rescued; we were transferred into a new realm and identity. "Brought into" (*methistēmi*) means a complete transfer of citizenship. The kingdom belongs to Jesus, the beloved Son, who shows His authority and deep, personal relationship with the Father (Philippians 3:20). This act gives us freedom.

Here, the term used is Apolutrou, emphasizing the liberation of a slave through monetary payment. This payment symbolizes the blood of Jesus shed on the cross. Forgiveness (aphesis) signifies the release or cancellation of a debt—sin is completely pardoned, not just overlooked.

Believers who please God are grateful. They live with gratitude, even during difficult times. Our entire lives should reflect thankful worship to the Father. Gratitude keeps us humble, joyful, and focused on grace rather than our own efforts. This helps us start and end each day by thanking God specifically for His work of redemption in our lives. You don't need to "qualify" yourself for God's love, inheritance, or acceptance. Salvation is based on God's work, not yours. This frees you from striving for approval and allows you to live in joyful obedience. When tempted to doubt your worth, declare aloud: "The Father has qualified me in Christ!"

Practicing gratitude is a powerful way to combat these tendencies. By focusing on even the smallest blessings and remembering God's provision, we can develop a heart of thankfulness, regardless of our circumstances. Paul shares the truth about gratitude by reminding us of the bigger picture.

Remembering that we are qualified to share in His inheritance should fill us with thankfulness. Amid our daily struggles, it's easy to forget that we have been instantly transferred from the domain of darkness to the kingdom of light. Paul reminds us that on our worst day, nothing can alter our inheritance in God's family.

Living a life that pleases the Lord by bearing fruit, growing in knowledge, being strengthened, and giving thanks is possible when we develop habits that allow the Holy Spirit to reveal God's will in practical ways as we draw closer to God and His plan.

Reflect & Respond

As you finish this chapter, take a few quiet moments to reflect on what God might be speaking to your heart. These questions help you remember key truths, deepen your understanding, challenge your assumptions, and motivate you to action. Whether you're working through them alone or with a group, invite the Holy Spirit to guide your thoughts, encourage honest conversations, and reveal the next step in your walk with Christ. Let this be not just a review but a response of faith, obedience, and transformation.

1. How do our perceptions of our earthly fathers influence our view of our heavenly Father, and how can a biblical understanding of God help correct any distorted perceptions?

2. What type of "fruit" is produced in a believer who abides in Christ and walks in the Spirit, and how does this fruit reflect a life that pleases God (Galatians 5:22-23)?

3. What is the difference between knowing about God and genuinely growing in the knowledge of Him? Additionally, why is it significant that the participle "growing" in Colossians 1:10 is passive?

4. How does walking in the Spirit empower believers to resist the desires of the flesh and align more fully with God's will?

5. Why does Paul emphasize patience and endurance as essential for a life that pleases God? How do these qualities promote our spiritual maturity?

6. In what areas do you see spiritual fruit, and where do you need to grow? What specific steps can assist you in reflecting more of Christ's character in those areas?

7. How has obedience shaped your growing relationship with God? Additionally, how would your life alter if you consistently perceived the world through the "filter" of God's presence and character?

8. How can cultivating a daily practice of gratitude help you overcome spiritual discouragement or feelings of inadequacy while also enhancing your spiritual growth and obedience?

CHAPTER NINE

LOOKING BACK

*Though I am not what I ought to be, I am not what I once was.
And by the grace of God, I am what I am.*
John Newton

As a young believer, I saw the listed habits as a way to make sure I was recognized by God (and others) as His child. Reading the Bible and praying were actions I believed should have made me acceptable to God. I didn't realize that being covered in Christ's righteousness already made me acceptable. The Christian life seemed more about avoiding sin than building a relationship. Success came from steering clear of cultural things the church considered wrong. When the Holy Spirit showed me my rigidity and Pharisaical attitudes, I began to see that God was inviting me into a relationship with Him. As I practiced these habits, I grew closer to Him. His will became clearer to me. It became important because I wanted to please Him in everything I did. Connecting renewing my mind with discovering His will not only brought me closer to the members of the Godhead but also changed me into the likeness of Jesus, ultimately pleasing God.

As I enter my eighty-third year, I see it differently than I did at thirty. I never made it into medical school. Looking back, I believe I would have been a good doctor, a modest believer, and a stranger to my wife of sixty-one years. Nothing immediately changed when I started applying Romans 12:1-2 to my life. However, as I developed the habit of renewing my mind over time, my thinking began to shift. As my perspective changed,

God revealed new insights. I started to see my wife with fresh eyes. Once again, the Bible became the central focus of my renewed life. God began planting seeds about being in "full-time ministry." Without realizing it, He was also transforming my wife. For over a year, we both prayed that God would call us into full-time ministry. My prayer included asking that He would guide LouAnna to the same conclusion. I later discovered she prayed for Him to lead me to that same path. God was changing our lives. We didn't know exactly where we were headed, but we were excited about the new changes. For us, "full-time ministry" seemed to be God's plan.

"Full-time ministry" is an interesting phrase. My dad was a successful businessman who taught that every believer is called to full-time ministry. Over time, this term has come to suggest that there are two groups of believers: one works a secular job and the other is paid for serving in a Christian ministry. My dad rejected this artificial division. He believed that the sacrifice of Jesus called for our full obedience and service. He was a Christian first and a businessman second. My dad was right. My path led me to become a pastor, but yours might take you in a different direction. No matter where you are in life, you are a full-time servant. Years ago, I was reminded that we all answer the question of who we are.

In the early 1970s, I was taking graduate classes in hospital administration. One course focused on what became known as "sensitivity training." Raised in conservative Christianity, I saw this class as a major tool of indoctrination from the opposing side. I heard that the class involved sitting in a circle and confessing all your hidden faults to strangers. It was filled with "warm fuzzy" words and thoughts, overflowing with "psycho-babble"—a term I often used to describe anything that vaguely resembled counseling.

By the time I reached Phoenix, I felt terrified. A friend who was driving with me shared my fears. "Have you heard anything about this class?" Before I could respond, he added, "I've heard they sit you in a circle and make you share about yourself with everyone. I'm not looking forward to this week!"

"That's it – I'm finished here!" I thought.

His fears intensified my own. When I arrived at the hotel where the class was held, I felt relief to see that the room was arranged with chairs and tables in a lecture style. Another person entering the room shared my relief, saying, "Oh good, there are tables!"

The instructor's arrival suddenly shattered our newfound peace. I looked at him and immediately disliked him. He was tall and thin, a sharp contrast to my pear-shaped figure. Tanned, extremely handsome, and with a full head of curly hair peeking out from beneath his sunglasses, he embodied the look I dislike. I hate it because I've tried to imitate it, only to fail. My head is too large, and when I try to place my sunglasses on my head (like cool people do), the frames warp so badly they never regain their shape. To make things worse, my skin and hair produce enough natural oil to qualify me as a potential member of OPEC. When I casually slide my sunglasses over my eyes, the oil smudges turn my glasses into opaque panes of glass.

This guy looked fantastic, just as I had imagined myself looking. And did I mention he was a former NBA player? As I scanned the room, I realized that every man saw him the same way. I also noticed that every woman had a completely different perspective. They were putty in his hands. Now, I really wanted to leave. Lecture or not, I couldn't spend a week listening to him. I nearly lost it when he made his first declaration.

"Oh, I didn't want any tables set up. Let's remove these tables and arrange the chairs in a circle."

I looked at the guy I had traveled with and realized he had emotionally detached from the world. Always being a somewhat compliant child, I helped arrange the chairs. I felt like someone tasked with tying the noose for his own hanging.

As the circle filled with victims, it was clear that the only enjoyable part of this experience would probably happen during the introductions. Having attended several of these classes, many participants in the room expected to answer the questions, "Who are you, and where do you work?"

Finally, the moment had arrived for class to start. People began taking their seats, glancing toward the instructor, who sat at the front of our circle, ready to begin. He carefully looked around the room and said, "Most of you are prepared to share who you are, where you're from, and what you do, but I'm not interested in that right now. I want to ask you one question: **'What is the most important thing about you that you want us to know?'"**

No one was prepared for this question. It felt like we had all been studying for a physics exam, only to find out that the first question was about Russian literature. As I thought it over, I said, "What a fantastic question!"

How would you respond to this? What is the most important thing you want us to know about yourself? Like my answer that day, yours will reveal something about you beyond your name and workplace.

Peter addresses this question at the start of his final letter to the churches in Asia Minor. In just nine words, he expresses the most important aspect of himself that he wants his readers to understand. He wrote this about four months before his death.

He wrote, "I am Simon Peter, a servant and apostle of Jesus Christ." (2 Peter 1:1) Do you see it? He wants us to understand three key points about him as he nears the end of his earthly life. First, he is Simon Peter. Simon was his given name, and Peter is the name he chose to embrace. He is a man in transition, becoming less Simon and more Peter. Second, he identifies as a servant first and then as an apostle. He aims to clarify that, above all, he is a servant. Third, he serves Jesus Christ, knowing Him personally. Word order is important. Peter writes "Jesus Christ" rather than the common title of Christ Jesus the Lord. Peter first knew Jesus as a friend and later came to believe that Jesus was the Christ.

This is not the same Peter we met at the beginning of the Gospels. Back then, he was rash and impulsive, outspoken and demanding—a diamond in the rough. He finished his life as a follower of Jesus, transformed and filled with the passion of someone who walks with Jesus every day. When you meet him, you meet Jesus. When he leaves a conversation with you, he takes a piece of Jesus with him. His life has a lasting impact. Even now, in our modern world, we reflect on and recognize the influence of Peter's life. We long for the same impact.

What does this look like? What makes Jesus' followers stand out in making a difference in the world? We are all "diamonds in the rough." Each of us has been rescued from the garbage heap to reflect the image of the one we follow. We have seen that these individuals, like Peter, have learned to be intentional in six key areas:

- They are being shaped into the image of Jesus.
- They embody God's priorities.
- They intentionally show God's will in their lives.
- They have implemented habits that renew their minds.
- They experience God's smile as they live the life they always wanted.
- They are making an impact in their world.

Observing their lives shows how they respond to the question, "What is the most important thing you want us to know about you today?" They reflect people who have decided to pick up their cross and follow Jesus. They understand that following Jesus requires a battle between committing to serve and follow, while resisting being shaped by the world's mold. They have developed the habit of renewing their minds to win this battle. When asked to describe the most important thing about themselves that they want others to know, they describe a life lived in the will of God — a life they have always hoped for.

Dallas Willard reminded us that "The most important aspect of your life is not what you do but who you become - that is what you will take into eternity." No matter your age or where you are as you read these final pages, it's never too late to make God smile. This is what you were created for, and doing so will bring the life you have always wanted.

To the man who pleases him, God gives wisdom, knowledge and happiness... (Ecclesiastes 2:26)

Reflect & Respond

As you finish this chapter, take a few quiet moments to reflect on what God might be speaking to your heart. These questions help you remember key truths, deepen your understanding, challenge your assumptions, and motivate you to action. Whether you're working through them alone or with a group, invite the Holy Spirit to guide your thoughts, encourage honest conversations, and reveal the next step in your walk with Christ. Let this be not just a review but a response of faith, obedience, and transformation.

1. Which scripture did the author start applying in his life that led to a significant transformation, and how has scripture influenced your spiritual growth?

2. How did the author's father define "full-time ministry," and do you agree with that perspective? Furthermore, how can that definition connect to your calling or daily life?

3. Which of the six signs of a transformed life resonated with you the most, and why is that area particularly meaningful in your journey with Christ?

4. If someone asked, "What is the most important thing we should know about you?" How would you respond, and does that response reflect a life transformed by following Jesus?

5. What immediate changes do you believe the Lord is calling you to make? What long-term changes will require intentional effort and growth over time to please Him?

6. Which spiritual habits have you found easiest to adopt, and which have you found most challenging? How has this book challenged or reshaped your understanding of what it means to live a Christian life?

APPENDIX

Start Building Habits
Bible Study Tools
Verses with *epiginosko* (true knowledge)

Start Building Habits

Establishing and maintaining healthy habits requires a combination of self-awareness, consistency, time management, and gradual changes. Self-awareness is shaped by various factors that influence how we understand ourselves and interact with the world. Here are some key factors that contribute to self-awareness:

1. Self-Reflection
Introspection is the ability to reflect on your thoughts, emotions, and actions. It enables you to analyze your experiences and understand how they influence your behavior. Journaling and recording your thoughts help clarify your emotions and actions by offering insights into your subconscious mind and thought patterns.

2. Emotional Intelligence (EQ)
Self-Perception: Understanding your emotions and their impact on your actions is essential to self-awareness. Individuals with high emotional intelligence are typically more attuned to their emotional states.

Emotion Regulation: The ability to manage and adjust one's emotions, particularly in challenging situations, is a vital component of self-awareness. Individuals who can effectively regulate their emotions often respond thoughtfully instead of reacting impulsively.

3. Feedback from Others
Constructive Feedback: Listening to feedback from others, whether positive or critical, helps you identify areas for growth and potential blind spots. It is important to seek feedback from trusted individuals who know you well.

Social Interactions: Interacting with others helps you understand yourself better by seeing things from their perspective, giving you new insights into your behavior and attitudes.

4. Mindfulness

Present-Moment Awareness: Mindfulness involves being completely present and engaged in the current moment instead of dwelling on past regrets or future worries. This practice helps you observe your thoughts and feelings without judgment, increasing awareness of your inner state.

Mindful Observation: Paying attention to your reactions in different situations, as well as noticing physical sensations, emotions, or thoughts, can enhance your awareness of your internal experience.

5. Values and Beliefs

Personal Values: Recognizing your core values (e.g., honesty, compassion, success) helps you determine if your actions match what matters most to you. Misalignment can cause dissatisfaction, while alignment enhances self-awareness and purpose.

Belief Systems: Your beliefs about yourself and the world shape how you see situations. Examining these beliefs—especially the limiting or unhelpful ones—can improve self-awareness and promote positive change.

6. Cognitive Biases

Self-Deception: Our biases, like self-serving bias or confirmation bias, can distort our judgment and block genuine self-awareness. Recognizing these biases helps you move beyond automatic assumptions and see yourself more clearly.

Cognitive Dissonance: The tension that occurs when our beliefs and actions don't match prompts us to reflect on our choices and adjust our behaviors, ultimately increasing our self-awareness.

7. Life Experiences

Past experiences: Your upbringing, relationships, and previous events influence how you see yourself and respond to others.

Reflecting on these experiences can uncover patterns in your thoughts and behaviors.

Challenges and Growth: Reflecting on personal challenges or periods of growth can improve self-awareness, as it often encourages you to confront your identity and how you have changed.

8. Personality Traits
Temperament: Your natural disposition, including traits like introversion versus extroversion, openness, and conscientiousness, influences how you see yourself and interact with others.

Self-Concept: The beliefs you hold about yourself—including your strengths, weaknesses, and identity—shape your self-awareness. A positive self-concept can foster personal growth, while a negative one may limit your awareness and potential.

9. Mindset
Growth Mindset: A mindset that embraces learning and change, rather than seeing abilities as fixed, can boost self-awareness. People with a growth mindset are more likely to reflect on their actions and keep improving.

Fixed Mindset: A fixed mindset can hinder self-awareness by reinforcing the belief that one's traits and abilities are unchangeable.

10. Self-Compassion
Kindness to Yourself: Being self-compassionate helps you to approach self-awareness without harsh judgment. Accepting your flaws and mistakes as part of being human encourages a healthy relationship with yourself, making it easier to find areas for growth.

11. Cultural and Social Influences
Cultural Identity: Your cultural background and the values you were raised with influence how you see yourself. Exploring how

culture shapes your identity can improve your self-awareness.

Social Comparison: Comparing yourself to others can motivate you; however, if done excessively or negatively, it can distort self-awareness. In contrast, healthy social comparison can help you recognize your uniqueness and find areas for growth.

12. Physical Awareness
Body Awareness: Paying attention to your body's signals, such as tension, fatigue, or relaxation, can offer insight into your emotional state and mental health. Practices like yoga, exercise, and body scanning can enhance physical self-awareness.

13. Purpose and Goals
Having a clear sense of purpose or direction in life helps you assess whether your actions align with your deeper goals and aspirations.

Goal Setting and Reflection: Establishing and reviewing personal goals encourages you to evaluate your progress and adjust your behavior, thereby boosting self-awareness.

Conclusion:
Self-awareness is a complex phenomenon influenced by numerous internal and external factors. By practicing mindfulness, engaging in self-reflection, seeking feedback, and challenging your beliefs, you can enhance your self-awareness and foster positive changes in your life.

Steps:
Start small and specific. Focus on one habit; instead of overhauling your lifestyle all at once, choose one area to improve. Set clear goals: make your habits specific.

Establish a routine by incorporating habits into your daily schedule: connect new habits with existing routines, plan them out, and add reminders or calendar entries to reinforce them.

Make it simple: Prepare ahead of time. Remove obstacles:

Minimize distractions or challenges that could stop you from following through.

Track your progress: Use a habit tracker, whether it's an app or a journal, to stay accountable. Celebrate small wins: Acknowledge your progress, no matter how small, to stay motivated.

Stay Consistent: Set a realistic time frame. Establishing a new habit can take anywhere from 21 to 66 days. Be patient with yourself. Avoid perfectionism: If you miss a day, don't give up. Focus on consistency rather than perfection.

Create a support system: Find an accountability partner and talk about your goals with someone who will motivate you. Join a community group: Surround yourself with people who share your objectives.

Adapt and adjust: Regularly review your progress. If a habit isn't sticking, identify the reason. Do you need to simplify it or try a different approach? Stay flexible: Life changes, so your habits may need to adapt to your circumstances. Be ready to make adjustments when needed.

Self-awareness involves recognizing your thoughts, feelings, and actions to make mindful decisions and foster personal growth. Here are steps you can take to enhance self-awareness. Practice Mindfulness: Engage in mindfulness activities like Scripture meditation, deep breathing, or body scans. These practices help you stay present and observe your thoughts and feelings without judgment. Over time, they can enhance your ability to recognize patterns in your thinking and reactions.

Self-Reflection: Regularly dedicate time for introspection. Ask yourself, "Why did I react this way?" or "What emotions am I feeling, and what triggered them?" Journaling can also be a helpful tool for self-reflection, providing insight into your experiences.

Seek Feedback: Ask trusted friends, family, or colleagues for their insights on how they see you. They may offer perspectives you haven't considered, helping you identify blind spots.

Observe Your Reactions: Pay attention to how you respond to different situations. Do certain triggers cause you to react impulsively or emotionally? Noticing these reactions can help you understand your usual responses and change them if needed.

Identify Core Values: Recognizing your core values helps guide your decisions and stay true to yourself. Reflect on what's most important to you and consider how you can live in harmony with those values.

Take personality and strengths assessments: tools like the Myers-Briggs Type Indicator (MBTI), StrengthsFinder, or the Enneagram can provide insights into your personality and natural talents. These assessments help you understand your tendencies and how you connect with others.

Create Space for Stillness: In the busy rush of life, it's easy to lose connection with your inner self. Consistently setting aside time for stillness or solitude can give you the space you need to reconnect and reflect on your experiences.

Challenge assumptions: Question your beliefs and assumptions about yourself and the world. Are they based on past experiences, or do they reflect your current self? Challenging deeply held beliefs can lead to a deeper understanding and personal growth.

Practice Emotional Awareness: Pay attention to your emotions throughout the day. Understanding why you feel a certain way can give you insight into your needs, desires, and fears. This can also help you manage your emotions more healthily.

Be compassionate with yourself: Developing self-awareness is a journey, and being patient and nonjudgmental toward yourself is essential. Growth takes time, and embracing mistakes as learning opportunities is crucial in cultivating a deeper understanding.

By consistently practicing these steps, you will begin to observe patterns in your thoughts, feelings, and behaviors, which will foster greater self-awareness and personal growth.

References on Habits:

Allen, T. A., & Kiburz, K. M. (2022). The value of emotional intelligence: Self-awareness, self-regulation, motivation, and empathy as key components. ResearchGate. https://www.researchgate.net/publication/379764627

American Psychological Association. (2023). How long does it really take to build a habit? Verywell Mind. https://www.verywellmind.com/how-long-does-it-really-take-to-build-a-healthy-habit-2224073

Baumeister, R. F., & Vohs, K. D. (Eds.). (2016). Handbook of self-regulation: Research, theory, and applications (3rd ed.). The Guilford Press.

Clear, J. (2018). Atomic habits: An easy & proven way to build good habits & break bad ones. Avery.

Creswell, J. D. (2017). Mindfulness interventions. Annual Review of Psychology, 68(1), 491–516. https://doi.org/10.1146/annurev-psych-042716-051139

Deci, E. L., & Ryan, R. M. (2000). The "what" and "why" of goal pursuits: Human needs and the self-determination of behavior. Psychological Inquiry, 11(4), 227–268. https://doi.org/10.1207/S15327965PLI1104_01

Duhigg, C. (2012). The power of habit: Why we do what we do in life and business. Random House.

Goleman, D. (2006). Emotional intelligence: Why it can matter more than IQ (10th anniversary ed.). Bantam Books.

Grant, A. M. (2007). Relational job design and the motivation to make a prosocial difference. Academy of Management Review, 32(2), 393–417. https://doi.org/10.5465/amr.2007.24351328

Kabat-Zinn, J. (2003). Mindfulness-based interventions in context: Past, present, and future. Clinical Psychology: Science and Practice, 10(2), 144–156. https://doi.org/10.1093/clipsy/bpg016

Neff, K. D. (2003). The development and validation of a scale to measure self-compassion. Self and Identity, 2(3), 223–250. https://doi.org/10.1080/15298860309027

Prochaska, J. O., & Velicer, W. F. (1997). The transtheoretical model of health behavior change. American Journal of Health Promotion, 12(1), 38–48. https://doi.org/10.4278/0890-1171-12.1.38

Ryan, R. M., & Deci, E. L. (2001). On happiness and human potentials: A review of research on hedonic and eudaimonic well-being. Annual Review of Psychology, 52(1), 141–166. https://doi.org/10.1146/annurev.psych.52.1.141

Tasha, E., & Eurich, T. (2018). Insight: The surprising truth about how others see us, how we see ourselves, and why the answers matter more than we think. Currency.

Wood, W., & Rünger, D. (2016). Psychology of habit. Annual Review of Psychology, 67, 289–314. https://doi.org/10.1146/annurev-psych-122414-033417

Bible Study Tools

Here are some tools for Bible study that can help you explore the Scriptures more thoroughly:

1. Bible Apps
YouVersion Bible App offers a variety of Bible translations, reading plans, and devotionals.
Logos Bible Software is ideal for in-depth study. It provides access to original language tools, commentaries, and a vast library.

Blue Letter Bible: Excellent for exploring Greek and Hebrew words, as well as different translations and commentaries.

2. Study Bibles and Books
The ESV Study Bible is celebrated for its comprehensive notes, maps, and articles that provide profound insights.

NIV Study Bible: Provides valuable contextual insights and concise, clear study notes.

How to Read Your Bible, by David and Renee Sanford.

Living by the Book by Howard G. Hendricks and William D. Hendricks.

3. Commentaries
Matthew Henry's Commentary is a classic work that offers valuable insights into the historical and theological aspects of each verse.

The Expositor's Bible Commentary provides scholarly insights and is used by many pastors and teachers.

The New International Commentary on the Old and New Testament is excellent for in-depth, academic-level study.

The Bible Knowledge Commentary

4. Concordances

Strong's Exhaustive Concordance is valuable for locating Bible verses by keyword and uncovering related passages.

Young's Analytical Concordance is an excellent resource for locating Hebrew and Greek words in the Bible.

5. Greek and Hebrew Tools
Strong's Lexicon: A valuable resource for studying the original languages of the Bible.
Interlinear Bible: This Bible displays the original Hebrew or Greek alongside the English translation, helping you study the original text.

6. Bible Dictionaries
Holman Illustrated Bible Dictionary: A thorough resource for understanding the cultural, historical, and geographical context of the Bible.

Anchor Bible Dictionary: This is one of the most esteemed Bible dictionaries, providing in-depth scholarly articles.

7. Bible Maps
Bible Atlas by National Geographic: Aids in visualizing the geography of biblical events.

The Zondervan Atlas of the Bible offers detailed maps and illustrations of significant biblical locations.

8. Bible Study Websites
Bible Gateway provides numerous translations, audio versions, and an easy way to look up verses and read daily devotionals.

Blue Letter Bible: Contains translations, Strong's Concordance, commentaries, and additional resources.

Bibleproject.com

9. Devotional Books
My Utmost for His Highest by Oswald Chambers: A timeless daily devotional that complements Bible reading beautifully.

New Morning Mercies by Paul David Tripp is a daily devotional that links Scripture with practical application.

10. Online Communities
BibleHub: Provides resources such as commentaries, lexicons, and verse searches, all in one location.

Reddit - Bible Study Group: A place for discussions and questions about Bible study.

epiginosko – True Knowledge

As I mentioned in the book, this word adds clarity to many passages. Listed below is a summary with my comments on each occurrence in the New Testament of this word. Here are the teaching implications of the use of this word in Scripture.

> All over the world this gospel is bearing fruit and growing, just as it has been doing among you since the day you heard it and <u>understood</u> God's grace in all its truth. (Colossians 1:6)

Paul reminds the Colossian Church that believing in the good news about Jesus Christ fosters a deeper understanding of God's grace. Without this belief, we can never truly comprehend God.

◆ ◆ ◆

> And this is my prayer: that your love may abound more and more in knowledge and depth of insight, 10 so that you may be able to discern what is best and may be pure and blameless until the day of Christ, 11 filled with the fruit of righteousness that comes through Jesus Christ—to the glory and praise of God. (Philippians 1:9-11)

Here, Paul reminds us that embodying and expressing authentic agape love is essential for gaining deeper understanding. This powerful idea emphasizes the immature struggle to tell right from wrong. In contrast, those who are spiritually mature naturally understand the differences between right and wrong and aim to distinguish between better and best. The answer is found in a few simple truths: we recognize the difference between better and best when our love "abounds" in genuine knowledge.

◆ ◆ ◆

> My purpose is that they may be encouraged in heart and united in love so that they may have the full riches of

complete understanding, in order that they may <u>know</u> the mystery of God, namely, Christ (Colossians 2:2)

Do not lie to each other, since you have taken off your old self with its practices and have put on the new self, which is being renewed in <u>knowledge</u> in the image of its Creator. (Colossians 3:9-10)

We must remember that Christianity has never been just a religion; it is a relationship. As Christians, we struggle between who we were before Christ and who we are becoming as God reveals the truth about our Creator each day.

◆ ◆ ◆

I pray that you may be active in sharing your faith so that you will <u>have a full understanding</u> of every good thing we have in Christ. (Philemon 6)

This is an interesting verse. Paul suggests a connection between sharing our faith and fully understanding all we have in Christ. When we don't share our faith, we deny others the good news and prevent ourselves from gaining a deeper understanding of everything we possess in Christ.

◆ ◆ ◆

. . . who wants all men to be saved and to come to a <u>knowledge</u> of the truth. (1 Timothy 2:4)

Those who oppose him he must gently instruct, in the hope that God will grant them repentance leading them to a <u>knowledge</u> of the truth, (2 Timothy 2:25)

always learning but never able to <u>acknowledge</u> the truth. (2 Timothy 3:7)

Paul, a servant of God and an apostle of Jesus Christ for the faith of God's elect and the <u>knowledge</u> of the truth that leads to godliness-- (Titus 1:1)

If we deliberately keep on sinning after we have received the <u>knowledge</u> of the truth, no sacrifice for sins is left, (Hebrews 10:26)

When our knowledge advances from basic principles to a deeper experiential awareness, we begin to understand the truth of God and His word in ways that connect us more closely to our Creator. Humanity asks: What is truth? This question can never be fully answered without a personal relationship with Jesus. Salvation is the only true way to know the truth and the God of truth. We teach those who refuse to accept the truth, hoping that "God will grant them repentance, leading them to a <u>knowledge</u> of the truth." Among them are false believers who are always learning but never truly grasp the truth at a deeper level. Knowing the truth more deeply is also the path to godliness. Without it, we risk falling into religious hypocrisy. The writer of Hebrews warns that if we continue to sin after gaining an *epiginosko* of the truth, we cannot go back and start over since Jesus' sacrifice has already paid the price for our sins. The implication is that we need to confess our sins and grow toward maturity.

◆ ◆ ◆

Therefore no one will be declared righteous in his sight by observing the law; rather, through the law we <u>become conscious</u> of sin. (Romans 3:20)

No matter how hard we try, we can never be right with God. Even obeying the Old Testament Law won't make us righteous before Him. The law makes us painfully aware of our sins. Recognizing our sin goes beyond just casually admitting that we are all sinners. A personal conviction causes sleepless nights until we settle things with Jesus.

◆ ◆ ◆

I keep asking that the God of our Lord Jesus Christ, the glorious Father, may give you the Spirit of wisdom and revelation, so that you may <u>know</u> him better. (Ephesians 1:17)

The Spirit offers wisdom and spiritual insight into God and His redemptive plan, which are vital for building a close relationship with Him.

◆ ◆ ◆

And we pray this in order that you may live a life worthy of the Lord and may please him in every way: bearing fruit in every good work, growing in the knowledge of God, (Colossians 1:10)

Grace and peace be yours in abundance through the <u>knowledge</u> of God and of Jesus our Lord. 3 His divine power has given us everything we need for life and godliness through our <u>knowledge</u> of him, who called us by his own glory and goodness. (2 Peter 1:2)

For if you possess these qualities in increasing measure, they will keep you from being ineffective and unproductive in your <u>knowledge</u> of our Lord Jesus Christ. (2 Peter 1:8)

until we all reach unity in the faith and in the <u>knowledge</u> of the Son of God and become mature, attaining to the whole measure of the fullness of Christ. (Ephesians 4:13)

Understanding God isn't enough. Knowing about God doesn't suffice. As Paul writes to the Church of Colossae, he emphasizes their need for a personal relationship with God, where He is most pleased when that relationship thrives. Peter underscores the importance of this connection, reminding us that joy and peace come through our relationship with the members of the Godhead. He indicates that joy and peace can't grow in our lives without this close bond. This relationship is the key to peace and joy and builds the foundation for living the life we've always wanted. By adding essential qualities for spiritual growth into our faith, we will consistently find our relationship with Jesus fulfilling and rewarding.

Paul reminds the Ephesian church that being equipped within the body of Christ is meant to nurture a deeper relationship with Jesus.

◆ ◆ ◆

If they have escaped the corruption of the world by knowing our Lord and Savior Jesus Christ and are again entangled in it and overcome, they are worse off at the end than they were at the beginning. (2 Peter 2:20)

For I can testify about them that they are zealous for God, but their zeal is not based on knowledge. (Romans 10:2)

Furthermore, since they did not think it worthwhile to retain the knowledge of God, he gave them over to a depraved mind, to do what ought not to be done. (Rom. 1:28)

I once believed that people with a deep understanding couldn't lose it. However, Peter reminds us that members of the early church had this knowledge and then abandoned it, joining the enemy's camp. This isn't new. Paul tells the Romans that there was a time when many understood God profoundly but chose to forsake that understanding to serve and worship false gods.

Rich Rollins, D.Min., is the co-author of *"Redeeming Relationships: How to Resolve 10 Common Conflicts and Reduce Their Frequency," "Spiritual Fitness: A Guide to Biblical Maturity," "Love Lock: Creating Lasting Connections with the One You Love," and "Putting a Smile on the Face of God: Simple Habits for a Life That Pleases Jesus."* He has worked as a healthcare professional, college vice president, executive pastor, university professor, and church consultant. Rich's broad church ministry and leadership experience have made him a popular counselor and consultant. He and his wife, LouAnna, have been married for more than sixty-one years and have two daughters and sons-in-law living in Southern California.

Join me in my biweekly Substack as we discover biblical truths.

www.ingramcontent.com/pod-product-compliance
Lightning Source LLC
LaVergne TN
LVHW051054080426
835508LV00019B/1866